Prophets / New

Prophets / Now

by
Leslie F. Brandt

with art by
Corita Kent

Publishing House
St. Louis

Other books by Leslie F. Brandt
Good Lord, Where Are You?
Great God, Here I Am
God Is Here—Let's Celebrate!
Psalms/Now
Living Through Loving
Epistles/Now
Praise the Lord!
Why Did This Happen To Me?
Jesus/Now

Concordia Publishing House, St. Louis, Missouri
Copyright © 1979 Concordia Publishing House
Manufactured in the United States of America

Library of Congress Cataloging in Publication Data

Brandt, Leslie F
    Prophets/now.

      1. Bible. O.T. Prophets—Meditations   2. Bible.
N.T. Revelation—Meditations.   I. Title.
BS1286.B7   242   79-4600
ISBN 0-570-03278-4

Contents

Preface

What if the ancient prophets were to pay us a visit today? What would they say to the millions of church members spread throughout our world? Speaking in the light of God's revealing through Jesus Christ, the prophets with their messages would reach beyond the people of Israel to the fulfillment of God's purposes and the final ingathering of His kingdom; but would their admonitions to us be that much different?

They would, of course, proclaim the Gospel of God's love and grace as it is revealed through the great Liberator, Jesus Christ. They would also note well the inconsistencies of modern-day believers in the ways in which they respond to the Good News of God's redeeming love.

Prophets/Now is one person's opinion of what they might say to each of us. It is this writer's hope that one or more of these prophets may speak to you.

Leslie F. Brandt

Isaiah 1

I am Isaiah.
I speak as I hear the Lord speak to those people
    and institutions that claim to be the new Israel,
    the blessed and redeemed children of God.
I speak to those who have heard the Word of God
    and to whom He has revealed His great love
    through His Son, Jesus Christ.
I speak to the multitudes of churches and parishes
    that abound in your land—
    the great congregations that gather in your cities,
    the little clusters of worshipers
    that come together throughout the countryside.
While the hosts of heaven rejoice over every person
    who is brought into the kingdom of God,
    my Creator and Lord is grieved over the faithlessness
    of many whose religion is confined
    to Sunday-morning confessions and proclamations.
I speak not to those who refuse to walk
    in the ways of God or sing His praises,
    those who make no pretense whatsoever
    to worship their Creator and Lord.
Many of these people are incorrigible and rebellious
    and are forging for themselves chains of darkness
    that shall bind them forever
    in their prisons of degradation and destruction.
I speak to those who assume
    that the religious exercises they perform
    or the words they speak identify them
    as the sons and daughters of the almighty God.

"You have had every opportunity to learn of Me
        and My purposes for your lives," I hear God say.
"You have been baptized into My kingdom
        and brought up within earshot of My Word and will.
You have sat at the feet of My prophets and apostles
        and have been ministered to by My priests and pastors.
I have revealed through My Son My eternal love for you,
        My redemption through His sacrifice on the cross,
        My gift of everlasting life
        through My raising Him from the dead,
        My ever-present grace through My Spirit
        that seeks to indwell
        and work out My purposes through you.
Yet many of you,
        while nodding your heads
        in acquiescence to
                My Word,
        have never yielded your hearts to My life
                and purposes.
Some of you continue to seek out My comfort
        or miracle-working power in the crises of your lives.
Others of you have left the God of your youth
        to pursue other idols that promise you much
        but grant you nothing.
Like foolish men who leave their true lovers
        to taste the forbidden fruits of harlotry,
        you have become estranged from the true and eternal
        to waste your lives and destroy your spirits
        with the sensational and materialistic things
        of your world.
There are very many within your churches
        who herald My name and Word
        and seek Me
        for what I can do to make them comfortable and happy—
        even for the assurance of eternal life—

but who have no regard for My ownership and control
        of their lives
    and little concern for their brothers and sisters
        about them
    and no intention whatever to take up the cross
    I would lay upon them on behalf of others.
For those who honor Me
    with their words but not their lives,
    who pay their respects but not their dues,
    who proclaim their love and loyalty on the day
        of worship
    only to live for themselves on other days of the week,
    who accept Me as Savior but not as Lord and King
        of their lives,
    for those I grieve because they are not living and acting
    as My servants in the world about them.
They do not take Me seriously;
    they do not worship Me honestly.
The exercises of worship they participate in—
    even the morality they acclaim
    and the good works they occasionally practice—
    do not fulfill My will for their lives.

"If it were not for those faithful few—
    and sometimes they are but a remnant—
    who are authentic in their faith and obedient in
        their living,
    who give Me and My purposes priority in their lives,
    who are committed to responding to My great love
    and dedicated to transmitting that love
    through their love for others,
    some of the religious activities
    that are promulgated by various churches
    would be repugnant.

Their robed choirs and great organs may stimulate
        congregations
    but such is not music to My heart.
Their proper liturgies and impressive pageantry
    will probably make people feel devout and religious
    without doing much to extend My kingdom
    or accomplish My purposes.
Even the Word that is preached,
    the sacraments administered, may be little more
        than hollow mockery
    if they do not proceed from and result in
    hearts and lives that are committed to My Word
    and My will as revealed through Jesus Christ.
If the people who gather
    to make their confessions and sing My praises
    do not feel lovingly compelled to carry out
        My objectives,
    to stand with the oppressed against their oppressors,
    to work for the dignity of every human being,
    to share their goods and gifts with those who are
        deprived,
    to accept and love their fellow persons
    even as they accept and love themselves—
    and to proclaim the love of God to those who
        will listen—
    then their worship is farcical
    and their relationship to Me very much in question.
I cannot listen to the prayers of those
    who do not love Me enough
    to embrace Me and My will for their lives.
I find no pleasure in the worship of those
    who make the things of the world their primary goal.
I will not grant My joy or power or assurance of
        life eternal
    to those who seek it for their comfort alone

and who refuse to respond to My love
by offering themselves as My servants of love
to the violent, hate-filled world about them.

"I call upon those of you who hear My Word
and sing My praises to repent of your sins,
to accept Me as your Lord and King,
to endure the risk and pain of servanthood
and to be the communicators and ministers
of My saving love and power to humanity around you.
I will blot out your iniquities
and cover up your wrongdoing
like the pure white snow that hides the filth
that accumulates in your cities.
I will forgive and forget your apathy and lethargy,
your sin and self-centeredness,
and restore you to My will and purposes for
your lives.
I will grant you My joy and fill you with My Spirit,
and I will work out My purposes through you.
I will listen to your prayers and accept your praises
and will impart to you the courage and strength
to confront the forces of evil
and extend My eternal kingdom
amidst the tempests and conflicts of your world.
I will go before you and will be with you
until your task is completed,
and you are forever united with Me
in the great kingdom for which you were created
and redeemed."

Isaiah 2 and 3

It is the depravity and the rebelliousness of humankind,
    of those creatures made in God's image
    who refuse to worship and obey their Creator,
    that is responsible for the darkness that pervades
        our world
    and the violence that tears it apart.
Our great God has in His wisdom seen fit
    to let it happen even while He watches over
    the victims of this world's atrocities
    and comforts and guides His children who walk
    within this world's darkness.
This shall not, however, go on forever.
There is coming a day,
    and it may be sooner than you think,
    when all this will be changed.
On that great day our God will break
    into this world's darkness and despair
    to reveal Himself as Lord and King.
It is on that day that He will gather
    the faithful of all lands into His kingdom
    and remove them forever from the pain and sorrow
        they endured
    in their wordly existence.
On that day He will bring judgment to bear
    upon the faithless and disobedient
    and take from them the power to wound one another
    and to dominate and destroy the world they inherited.
On that day wars will cease;
    the erratic forces of nature will be contained and
        controlled;

nations and their citizens will know and fear
the God they rebelled against or simply ignored.
It is on this day that everyone and everything
that has stood up against the God of creation
shall be brought low.
Those who have defied Him
will now scamper in terror before Him;
they shall seek out fortresses and places of darkness
that they might hide from Him.
It will be a frightful day, indeed,
for those selfish, arrogant creatures
who lived only for the material things of this
world
and who plundered God's rich gifts
as well as the lives and property of their
fellow beings
in order to quench their insatiable desires.
What a day of joy it will be, however,
for those who suffered and faithfully served
as the sons and daughters of the invisible,
omnipotent, and everywhere present God!
The day of the Lord is near at hand;
the Lord is about to judge His people.
It will be a day of celebration
for those who faithfully followed Him
and who sacrificially served their fellow beings
in the world about them.
For those who deprived others of their gifts
and rights
and oppressed their human peers—
in order to live in luxury and indifference,
to gain power and glory for themselves—
it will be a sad and bitter day.

Isaiah 6—8

It was while in the throes of self-pity and
        depression—
    even while I was questioning God's concern for me
        and my world—
    that I was permitted a unique experience.
I do know that I was struck, as if by lightning,
    with the frightening realization that God
    was near to me, that He was speaking to me—
    putting thoughts into my head
    that almost paralyzed me with fear.
I saw nothing, but I felt
    as I had never felt before—unworthy, guilty,
        ashamed—
    yet strangely awed, amazed, overcome
    by some inexplicable, out-of-this-world Presence,
    that blotted out for the moment all that was associated
    with natural life on this planet.
As if propelled by some invisible force,
    I flung myself to the ground—clawing blindly
    at the sticks and stones that lay about me.
Then all doubts dissolved;
    all questions dissipated like smoke in the wind;
    the conflicts and problems that brought me
    to this hour suddenly vanished;
    it was as if nothing upon this earth existed—
    and nothing else mattered—
    except that precise moment in the presence
    of this indefinable, indescribable Power
    that permeated and filled the emptiness around me.

And it was at this moment—
    in the midst of this powerful Presence—
    that I sensed an overwhelming love, a recognition,
    an acceptance as a creature of God, forgiven,
        redeemed, beloved.
My feelings of shame and unworthiness
    were drowned in a sea of joy and peace,
    and I knew in a way that I had never known before
    that I was a son and servant of the living God.
A deep, profound conviction began to take shape in my heart,
    that as God's son and servant I was to be
    weighed down with a tremendous responsibility—
    the task of bringing God's Word of judgment and grace
    to the people about me.
Before I could proclaim the glad tidings of His
        redeeming love,
    I must prepare people with the message of His
        judgment—
    revealing to them their blindness and indifference,
    their rebelliousness and unrighteousness,
    the emptiness of their lives and the self-centeredness
        of their living.
Only then would those who heard
    the piercing Word of judgment be prepared to hear
    the blessed message of God's loving grace.
And what a message it was—
    the word of divine forgiveness,
    of the power of regeneration and restoration,
    the gift of eternal life—
    of God's acceptance of His repentant creatures
    as revealed through His Son, who,
    coming to this world as man-born-of-woman,
    took upon Himself the guilt and consequences
    of humankind's sin and rebelliousness
    in order that men and women might be
        reconciled to their God!

This is what actually happened in our universe.
God's creatures could not come to Him—
    so fractured were their lives, so dead their spirits.
Their religious exercises
    made no impression upon Him whatever
    and were, in reality, foolhardy attempts
    to cover up their inner wickedness.
Thus God came to humankind—
    implanting Himself in the womb of one of His creatures
    and coming forth as the Christ, God's Son,
        humanity's Savior.

There were other convictions that began to take shape
    in my thoughts and feelings.
I was not to compromise my ministry
    by passing out shallow words of false comfort
    to disobedient and unbelieving people.
I was not to be afraid of the consequences of my
        servanthood
    and the sufferings it would engender for me.
I was never to seek for strength or guidance
    from anything or any other than God alone
    and those servants that He would use
    in His working within my life.
Nor was I to glory or rest securely
    in my unique experience—
    or even to seek other such experiences.
I was commanded to walk in faith
    and to serve in obedience according to the Word
    that He had given to me.

Isaiah 9 and 11

That One who has come
      is about to return—to come again.
He came out of the nation of Israel;
    He came to save, to judge,
    to rule over the people of this world.
He came as a child born of woman
    and was brought forth out of poverty and pain.
He was from God and, in His humanity,
    was filled with the Spirit of God, His Father.
He came to bring the light of God
    into a dark and violent world.
He came to set men and women free
    from the bondage of sin
    and the burdens that weighed them down.
He came to bring salvation to the children of God,
    to judge the wickedness of God's
    self-centered
        and rebellious creatures,
    and to establish a new kingdom
    of light and joy and righteousness.
He took upon Himself the sins of humankind
    and was put to death upon a cross
    only to be raised from the dead
    and to return to His Father.
His invisible Spirit now abides within the hearts
    of God's redeemed children
    to comfort and guide them through the dark corridors
        of a disjointed world.
Thus He has come;

in reality, He has never left this world.
He continues to walk among His faithful followers,
    granting them courage and strength and joy,
    and is working out the purposes of His Father
        through them.

The day is soon upon us—that day
    in which the kingdom of God will be fully revealed.
In that day that One
    who has come to save His people from their sins
    will judge the world in its wickedness.
The kingdom of God will blaze forth
    in all its power and glory.
The darkness of this world will give way
    to the dawn of a new day.
Violence will cease;
    the spiritual forces of darkness will be subdued;
    the righteousness of God will prevail
    in and over the lives of all His creatures.
In that day the earth shall be filled
    with the knowledge of God.
Whereas the wicked shall be terrified
    and seek out for themselves places in which
        to hide,
    the redeemed will welcome with joy
    the appearance of their King.
There will be peace and order and righteousness
    among people and nations.
All that is evil—the lies and deeds,
    the hypocrisy and compromises,
    the ugliness that now abounds—will be exposed.
Our great God will exercise full control
    of the world He created—
    gathering His faithful children to Himself
    and casting forever his arrogant, hate-filled,

unbelieving creatures into the pits of darkness
they created for themselves.
Time is running out;
the day of the Lord is soon upon us.

Isaiah 12

What a day that will be—the day of the Lord!
On that day the hearts of God's children
    will be filled with thanksgiving.
While the unbelieving and arrogant
    will cringe in fear or run in terror,
    the sons and daughters of God will not be afraid;
    they will fill the air with praises
    to the God of their salvation.
They will sing songs of joy
    and bravely exalt His name throughout all the world.
Their lives will be filled with love
    and they will truly love one another.
They will embrace each other
    as sisters and brothers in the great family of God.
There will no longer be poor or rich, black or white,
    nor will people be separated
    by denominational doctrines or traditions.
All who have been found by God through Christ
    will be united in love and joy
    as the children and servants of that God
    who is now fully revealed.
Those who claimed their freedom from sin
    through their loving Redeemer
    will now know that freedom totally,
    and they will be set free from the evil
        that tempts,
    the suffering that inhibits, the fears and doubts
    that once obscured their God.

Now and forever,
    they are the inhabitants of the new kingdom,
    the kingdom of righteousness and joy and love.
The darkness has forever been dispelled,
    and they shall sing and shout for joy
    as the beloved children of God.

Isaiah 17:10-14

I am greatly concerned about those of you
    who were reared in the true faith
    and were faithfully taught about your Creator
        and Redeemer.
You saw no reason to doubt
    what was proclaimed to you in your early years,
    and you found joy and security in the love of God
    as revealed through Jesus Christ.
As you grew older, however,
    confronting the pains and problems
    that afflict all of God's creatures,
    and tempted by the glitter and dazzle of this world's
        foolish toys,
    you drifted away from the God of your youth
    to search for other gods that appeared to have
        ready answers
    for your problems or immediate sustenance
    for your crying needs.
Or you felt that the God about whom you were taught
    was only a childhood crutch
    and you no longer needed this childish fantasy—
    that you could make it on your own
    with just a little help from your friends.
O, the arrogance of God's creatures
    who put Him aside for the cheap, tantalizing
    thrills of earthbound living!
Like gamblers,
    they invest small pieces of their lives in this or that,
    always seeking but never being found by that One

who came to fill the emptiness of their inner spirits—
that One they turned away from in their search
for identity and fulfillment among the gods or idols
that appeal to their depraved instincts and desires.
They wander about like dazed zombies,
pushed about by physical need or circumstances
as clouds are moved by the winds.
Some of these people,
because of the patience of their ever-loving God,
do find the way back to their first-love—
to that One they knew as children.
They are restored to their heavenly Father
and become, once more,
the recipients of His saving love.
There are others, many others,
who are never brought back to that faith
they were once taught.
They will wander forever in that abject darkness
in which they have immersed themselves,
concocting gods of their own that can never meet
the genuine needs of their lives.

Isaiah 25—26:14

I rejoice in the knowledge
   that our God has not absented Himself from
      our world—
   and this despite the evil and arrogance
   that dominates the lives
   of so many of His creatures.
He will have the last word—
   even while He allows His wayward children
   to set themselves against Him
   and His purposes for their lives.
Men and women have built cities and established nations
   that have become fortresses of evil
   and breeding places for crime and injustice.
Its citizens have become enslaved to their own lusts,
   held in bondage by their own selfishness,
   indifferent to the plight of the poor
   and the oppressed about them.
Their leaders have set themselves up as gods over their
      subjects—
   using their power to pursue their own ungodly objectives.
But God has not forsaken His children.
He continues to be concerned about the poor
   and about those who suffer
   under the oppression of wicked rulers.
He promises that earthly fortresses will crumble,
   that cities will fall into ruin,
   that nations will be dissolved,
   and all that fails to measure up to God's plan
   will be demolished.

He promises, as well, another kind of city
    where wickedness will not be permitted to exist.
It will be a kingdom of beauty and goodness,
    joy and righteousness.
The poor will be enriched, the faithful blest,
    in this new kingdom.
There will be no wars;
    oppression and poverty will not be known.
God will be God;
    men and women will be the beloved children of God.
The citizens of this great city—this kingdom—
    will be at peace with God and with one another.
There shall no longer be fear or doubt;
    people will not seek advantage or power over
        each other.
It will be a place of joy forever.

Ah, how we long for such a time
    when God's promises will be fulfilled,
    when the pride of egocentric men and women
    will be brought low, and our Creator's plans
    will be consummated for those who are faithful
        to Him!
How much we would wish
    to dwell in a city where righteousness reigns supreme
    and where crime and corruption are forever abolished!
It shall come to pass; it shall come to pass.

Isaiah 29 and 30

It is not surprising that people cannot see
     what God has done for them,
     or understand the Word He has committed to them.
They are blinded by the fool's gold of this world
     and seduced by the high-sounding wisdom
     of this ephemeral existence.
Their spirits numb
     to the transcendent message of their Creator,
     they embrace those philosophies and follow those leaders
     that promise instant happiness,
     and they sell out their lives
     for a pocketful
          of stones.
Even many of those
     who hear of God's forgiving and saving love
          through Christ
     lip-worship Him for what He can do for them
     while feasting their lives on the cheap husks
     of this temporal existence.
Created by God to be the objects of His love,
     they turn from Him to follow their own pursuits
     and seek out their own objectives.
They float aimlessly
     within the orbits of their own making
     and many of them will be lost forever
     within the darkness and nothingness of this universe.
There are those, however,
     who shall be sought after and found by the God
          of the universe

and restored to a loving relationship with Him.
They shall be enabled to see His glory,
    to sense His love, and will rejoice forever
    in His kingdom of righteousness.
Whereas they shall continue to face up with adversity
    as long as they are in this world,
    they shall walk in joy, for they know
    that God walks with them and goes before them
    and is drawing them to that great Day
    when they will weep no more
    and all that is bright and joyful and abundant
    will reign forevermore.

Isaiah 31:1-6

Nations rely on their military machines
    to deter foreign enemies
    or to secure and sustain their power
    over threatening forces within their boundaries.
People reach out to foreign spiritual powers
    or mystical philosophies
    for courage and meaning in life
    when they are confused or frightened.
There are all kinds of idols
    that human beings pull out and polish up
    to help them through some crisis or other in
        their lives.
There are few, however,
    who turn their faces toward their Creator and God
    for His counsel and guidance in times of trouble.
Even many of those
    who do frantically resort to prayer
    often seek to use God for immediate comfort and aid
    without any intent to live within His will for
        their lives.
Our Lord will watch over those who trust in Him.
He will not always shield His children
    from life's troubles, but He will circumscribe them
    with His love and fortify them with His grace
    against the enemies that assail them.
He will give His children the final victory
    over those who seek to destroy them.
All those who will rely upon the God of their creation—
    in times of joy or sorrow, sunshine or darkness,

calm or conflict—
will discover that His grace is sufficient;
and He will sustain them
whatever the trials and tribulations
that come their way.

Isaiah 40

The Lord comes to judge the nations of this world;
    He comes, as well,
    to give hope and comfort to His people.
Let us prepare the way for His coming into our lives.
We are to do this by opening our hearts to Him.
There are the valleys of emptiness,
    gaping holes created by our vain endeavors
    to find meaning and purpose for our lives
    apart from a believing and loving relationship
        to God.
We have dug these great excavations
    in our frenzied attempts
    to find soul peace and divine order
    and have, instead, found fool's gold.
There are the mountains
    we have raised up to hide us
    from the piercing and all-knowing countenance
    of the Lord.
They are forbidding obstacles
    to our Lord's coming into our lives
    for He will not yet step over the molehill
    or leap the mountain of our obstinance or
        disobedience
    except we surrender them to His purging and
        removal.
There are those crooked paths that we have traveled
    in our pursuit of wealth or pleasure or fame.
We cannot fill up those valleys
    or tear down those mountains

or straighten those crooked paths
by our efforts alone;
we can only recognize them, be appalled over them,
and allow the Lord to deal with them
through His power and grace.
And deal with them He will.
He comes to bring us back to Himself,
to forgive us for our hardness of heart,
our selfishness and rebelliousness.
He comes to fill our valleys of despair
with joy
and hope,
to turn our mountain of obstacles
into pillars
of strength.
to guide us along straight paths
that lead to eternal meaning and fulfillment.
He comes to reveal His glory and immortality
over against the temporality and ephemerality
of the world about us.
He comes to care for His own—for those
who embrace Him as Savior and worship Him as Lord.
He, who is far greater
than the universe He created
and before whom the power of great nations
is but empty wind,
has come to grant strength to those who are weak
and courage to those who are afraid,
thus enabling His faithful children
to stand strong and firm
against those forces that seek to confuse them
and threaten to destroy them.

How full of wonder and splendor is our God!
How beautiful His created world in which we live!

Yet even this world which He created
    and the atmosphere which surrounds it
    shall not last forever.
Like the flowers that fade and die
    so will the majesty and beauty of creation about us
    fade away into nothingness.
Only God, His word of judgment, His loving salvation,
    shall be forever.
He who is greater than all we can imagine,
    who created humankind out of dust,
    and makes the sun and the stars light our dark paths,
    who gives us mountains to stand guard over us,
    oceans and lakes to sustain us,
    fruits and vegetables to feed us,
    trees to shade and shelter us,
    the furs and skins of animals to clothe us,
    fuel to warm us,
    He is far greater than all of His gifts to us.
How dare we worship the gifts that are perishable
    rather than their Creator-God who is forever?
It is He who reigns over the earth
    and far above and beyond this world.
It is He who reaches down to His children,
    to gather them together
    as a shepherd gathers his sheep
    and brings them into the fold.
He is the One who is strong and almighty and ever-loving,
    who gives strength to the weak
    and power to the powerless,
    who saves and keeps forever those who hear
    and who embrace His blessed Word.
How full of wonder and splendor is our God!

Isaiah 41 and 42

Do you not understand,
    you who are the redeemed children of God,
    who have been restored to His saving grace,
    that you are now and forever His beloved servants?
You did not choose Him or seek Him out;
    He chose you and sought you out.
You did not win His favor through your good behavior.
You offended, betrayed, ran away
    from the God of your creation
    and took refuge in the foolish pleasures
    and false promises of this world.
While you deserved nothing less than His fierce judgment,
    He pursued you into the darkness and emptiness of
        your silly lives
    to draw you back to Himself.
He did all this because He loved you
    far more than you could love your offspring—
    and because He wanted you back in His family again.
Because you are His children you are blessed
    with the honor and privilege of being His servants.
You have no wisdom or strength in yourselves
    to qualify you for servanthood—
    or to enable you to carry out the purposes
    of your Creator-God in your world.
He has, nevertheless, chosen you, redeemed you,
    and promised to grant you the courage and wisdom
    and strength necessary to be His faithful emissaries
        on your planet—
    His voice of judgment, His messengers of salvation,

His vessels of love and power
to His loveless and powerless creatures about you.

As His beloved servants,
you are objects of His joy and delight.
The paths you travel will not be smooth;
there will be enemies to face and failures to contend with.
The people you are to serve,
distracted as they are
by the glitter of this world's tinsel
and immersed in their own egocentric objectives,
will not always be prepared for the message of
God's love
nor will they receive with gratitude His Word
of judgment
upon their nefarious activities.
Nevertheless, you have been endued
with the Spirit of your God.
You will be upheld by His might and power.
You have been promised the ultimate victory
over all the foes of His kingdom—
and the ever-present joy
of knowing that you are His children and servants
carrying out His purposes in your world.
Thus with conviction and courage you can speak
of God's infinite love,
and you can demonstrate such love in your struggles
to bring light to those in darkness,
freedom to the oppressed, sustenance to the deprived,
and dignity, opportunity, and justice
for all of God's human creatures in your
generation.
Rejoice in your God! Sing His praises!
for you are His beloved and blessed servants!

Isaiah 43

The Lord who spoke to His own in past centuries
    speaks to His creatures whom He has created
    and redeemed in this century.
"You need not be afraid," He would say to you.
"I have forgiven your sin;
    I have reconciled you to Myself;
    I have chosen you and adopted you as My children;
    I love you and I will honor you.
Even when you are battered
    by the storms that rage about you or are pressured
    by the forces of evil that threaten you,
    I will be close to you and bear with you
    the sufferings and persecutions that afflict you.
The gods that others worship and cling to
    cannot make such promises,
    for I, alone, have been and always shall be God,
    and I have chosen you to be My servants.
As long as you worship and serve Me
    there is nothing that can take you away from Me.
I am your God; remember that.
Even when you foolishly strayed
    from My will for your lives
    to slake your thirst or satisfy your hunger
    from foreign and impure sources—
    only to discover that such could not fulfill
    what was promised—I reached out in love
    to take you back to Myself,
    to blot out your sins and restore you to My purposes.
I created you to abide within My will for your lives.

You will find true joy and eternal satisfaction
only as you walk in the paths
that I have set before you."

Isaiah 47

There are many who turn away from the God of their
        creation.
They seek their comfort in the inanimate objects
    that abound about them.
They look for guidance in the stars that shine upon them.
They submit to sorcerers and charlatans who, for a price,
    promise to reveal the future to them.
Some people find their joy
    in the passing pleasures of this world
    or rest secure in the wealth they take from others.
Or they assume they are the center of their world
    and everything that exists
    revolves around them and is designed to serve them.

They may, indeed, find a measure of contentment—
    for a day or a year—
    but there comes a time when everything
    in which they have invested will crumble
    and come tumbling down around them.
They have no God to lead them through raging waters
    or consuming fires.
The stars above will not cast light upon their dark nights;
    the paths they travel lead to endless deserts
    of emptiness and despair.
They have chosen to ignore the God of their creation;
    the sorcerers they have chosen to follow,
    or the self-will they have elected to glorify,
    brings them no counsel or comfort
    when the sky falls in upon them.

Isaiah 51:6-13

Woe be to those who make all their investments
    in those things they can count or who pin their lives
    only upon that which they can comprehend.
It has been assumed
    that the earth will ultimately vanish and
    that all living creatures will eventually die.
Now it has become understood, even by small minds,
    that the world which sustains us
    is gradually wearing out like an old garment,
    that its rich resources are rapidly being drained away.
Only the God who gave us our world is forever—
    and so are those whom He redeems and has promised
    to keep forever.
Thus it is only as the objects of His great salvation
    that we can rest in the promise and gift of eternal life.
Those who put their trust in God
    need not fear the gradual disintegration of the world
    nor the persecution and oppression
    perpetuated by men who flaunt their wealth and prestige
    as rulers of the world.
They know that the God who created the heavens and the
        earth
    and men and women to dwell upon the earth,
    and who provides that which is necessary
    to sustain life upon the earth
    is able to keep and comfort His children.
It is this God who will inhibit the forces of evil
    and restrain the oppressor and who will,
    in His own time, deliver His sons and daughters

from all the sufferings and sorrows
that have plagued them in this world.
Arise and stand tall, sons and daughters of God!
Cast out your fear and trust in your heavenly Father!
You belong to Him forever.

Isaiah 52

How blessed are those who are chosen
    to be the servants of God!
What a message they have to proclaim
    concerning God's love for the human family!
Not only do they speak of God's judgment, but,
    endued with His Spirit
    and authorized and empowered by His saving grace,
    they are to make known His salvation,
    to spread the glad tidings of His redeeming and
        reconciling love
    to all who will listen to His gracious Word.
It is true!
God will judge and condemn to eternal darkness
    all who persist in opposing Him and His purposes.
It is equally true that those who deserve nothing less—
    who have rebelled against their Creator-God
    and broken His law and have worshiped and lived
    for the things of this world—
    that they can be redeemed from the pits
    of darkness and be reconciled to God once more.
We who are now God's children and servants
    were once the children of darkness and disobedience.
God sought us, found us, and took us back to Himself.
Now we are enjoined and assigned to live out and proclaim
    the redeeming and reconciling love of our God
    to our fallen, lost, suffering sisters and brothers
    throughout our world.
It is a joyous task, a tremendous responsibility,
    an exciting adventure,

a difficult and pain-filled struggle.
We plunge forth with confidence—
    and with the assurance that our great God has
        circumscribed us
    with His love and care
    and that we are His precious vessels,
    His children and servants forever.

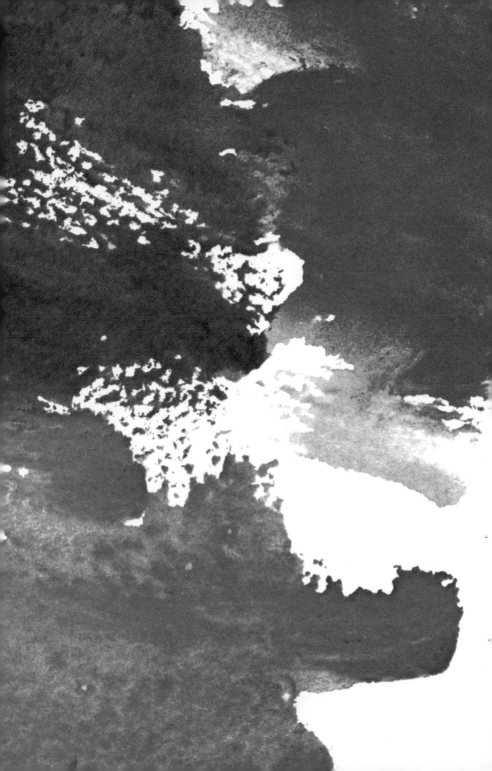

Isaiah 53:1-12

Our great God has revealed Himself to us.
Miraculously conceived within a human creature,
    He came to us as man-born-of-woman.
Brought forth amidst poverty, He grew up among the poor.
There were no fine silks or shining crowns to adorn Him.
People never bowed before Him in fear or even assumed
    that He was different from them.
He had not come to be an earthly ruler
    nor to strive for worldly acclaim.
He had come to reveal the love of his Father, our God,
    and to manifest His great power amidst the paltry
    riches and foolish might of earthbound rulers.
He came to accomplish that which was totally contrary
    to everything His peers would expect of a ruler or king.
It is no wonder that He was scorned, despised,
    rejected by His neighbors
    and ultimately destroyed by the religious leaders.
They could not understand His teachings
    concerning a heavenly kingdom
    and saw little need for anything beyond
    the solving of their own small problems.
They did not accept Him as God-revealed
    or the Messiah that had been promised.
Thus they ignored Him or regarded Him
    as some silly fanatic
    who was simply blowing His own trumpet
    and seeking gain for Himself.

It was through Him, however, that God came to us.
He came not as avenger of humankind's evils,
    but as a lover of God's fallen creatures—

a Savior of the human family.
He experienced the poverty of those around Him
    and knew well the poverty of their spirits.
He felt our pain, our grief, our oppression.
He identified with our human weaknesses.
He healed many of our sicknesses
    and taught us about God's love
    and our hope of becoming God's beloved children
    through His life and teaching.
But He did more—much more.
He suffered for our sins;
    He took upon Himself the guilt of our iniquities.
Rather than ascending a throne as ruler,
    He was put to death as a criminal.
He who judged us as sinners came to us
    as man-born-of-woman
    to take upon Himself His own judgment
    upon our Lawbreaking and sinfulness.
He was in our midst as God-man and we,
    victims of our self-righteousness,
    offended by His righteous condemnation of our sins,
    scorned His love,
    put down his proclamations of salvation,
    and cruelly persecuted and executed Him.
Instead of hell itself opening up to receive us,
    the very death of this righteous One became our death
    and opened the gates to eternal life
    for all those who would embrace in faith this God
    who came to us in Jesus Christ.
This is the manner in which God,
    whom we could never reach,
    came to us and made it possible for us to know and
        experience his righteousness—
    to be set free from sin's bondage
    and to be reconciled to His kingdom forever.
How great is God's love for His wayward children!

Isaiah 55

The love of a righteous God
    is not something to be bought;
    it is a gift to be received.
You are invited to plunge into the waters of life,
    to partake of God's feast of good things,
    not as something earned
    because of your efforts or endeavors,
    but because of God's love for you
    and His incessant desire to bring you
    into His kingdom.
Why is it that multitudes continue
    to focus their lives and talents
    and expend their strength and energy upon those things
    that cannot meet their deepest longings
    nor grant them infinite joy?
Those who are attracted and betrayed
    by the glitter of this world will go their way—
    even God cannot keep them from such foolishness
    if that is their choice.
You, however, do not have to accompany them—
    or follow them.
You are summoned by the King of kings,
    the God of your creation,
    to embrace that for which you were created,
    His righteousness, His saving grace, life eternal,
    as His sons and daughters.
God, through that One whom He has sent,
    His very Son, our Lord, has made that possible.
There is nothing to bring, no sacrifice to be offered,

no merits to be earned,
all this has been done on your behalf.
You need only to come, to partake, and to live forever
in the light and joy of God's love and favor.

Isaiah 61

The Spirit of God, who was upon
    and within the God-man, Jesus Christ, now abides
    within all those who are the redeemed children
    of their Creator-Father.
The task that the Christ was given to fulfill
    has now become the task and objective
    of His faithful servants.
This is to proclaim the good news of God's saving love,
    the forgiveness of sin,
    and the gift of everlasting life,
    as well as being the vehicles of His rich gifts
    to those who are in need of such.
There is healing for those who are afflicted,
    comfort for those who mourn,
    freedom for those who are under bondage.
This is what God's servants are enjoined to proclaim
    and to make happen.
These things will begin to happen when, guided by His
        Spirit,
    Christians commit themselves to the blessed task
    of channeling God's love and freeing power
    to the suffering and oppressed about them.

God's servants ought not to be concerned about rewards;
    their obedience to their God and Father
    is their response to the love of God
    that was poured out upon them.
They may seldom be rewarded by the people they serve;
    indeed, as with Christ,

they may be persecuted for their good works.
Nevertheless, there will be rewards
    for those who are faithful.
They will, in God's own time,
    be honored as His beloved servants.
Those who serve their fellow persons
    as authorized and sent by God are the only hope
    for the floundering masses of this world
    for they proclaim the Word and saving power
    of their Creator-God.
And they proclaim the single and glorious hope
    for what lies beyond this world—the kingdom
    of the living God.
It is in that kingdom that God's children and servants
    will be honored and rewarded
    with everlasting life and joy.

Jeremiah 1 and Lamentations 3

I am Jeremiah.
Even when I was very young
    I knew that God's hand was upon me,
    that I was destined to be His son and servant
    all the days of my life.
While my peers about me were, like butterflies,
    flitting from flower to flower seeking out
    and relishing the sweet honey of this world,
    pursuing the thrills and delights of this existence,
    I was marked for better things
    and set aside for other purposes.
It is true,
    God did reveal Himself to me in very convincing ways,
    through His Word that is available to all His creatures—
    and through the thoughts of my heart.
"I have sought you out; I have chosen you,"
    I heard Him say.
"Even before you were born
    I knew that you were to be consecrated to Me and My
        objectives
    in your world."
I sensed no special gifts
    and was not aware of anything I possessed
    that would be of value to God.
"Never mind! What I require of you I will enable you
    to accomplish on My behalf," He said to me.
"I will put My words in your mouth, My thoughts
    into your mind, My gifts into your hands,
    My courage into your heart,

and I will instruct and guide you in the way
	you are to go.
Do not be afraid! only walk in faith
	and in obedience to My will for you."

I was much younger then,
	and despite my family and friends, who regarded me
	respectfully, yet laughingly, as some religious fanatic,
	I bravely and joyfully overcame my doubts and fears
	and even confronted with scorn the obstacles
	that stood in my way.
In my zeal to be a faithful servant of God,
	I did some foolish things, but, all in all,
	I continued to walk in the path that He set before me
	and to expend my youthful energy in what I assumed
	to be His objectives.

That was many years ago.
I am much older now and, at times,
	not nearly so certain that I was chosen
	even from birth to be a servant of God—
	and not nearly as enthusiastic about serving Him
	among my peers.
It may be because my failures far outnumber
	any successes I may claim in my lifetime of
		service—
	that people around me are still flitting
	like butterflies from flower to flower
	savoring the delights of this existence
	with scarcely a thought about God
	and His will for their lives or about eternity
	and its ultimate demands upon God's creatures.
The church I grew up with and am a part of today
	does not appear to be as significant and far-reaching
	as it was in my youth,

and masses of people are seeking to meet their
    spiritual needs—
or get their transcendent kicks—
within consciousness-raising therapy groups
that lead them to independence and self-reliance
rather than to their Creator-God.
Gimmicks appear to take over or to take the place of God,
    and new kinds of idolatry have replaced
    the brass idols and symbols of past centuries.
Even the God-inspired Scriptures that nurtured my life
    are often utilized to create sects and cults
    that pacify people with heavenly promises
    while anesthetizing them to the challenge
    and responsibility of sacrificial service.
Though there are glorious exceptions,
    the brash, redundant, constant promotion of the Gospel
    that dins the ears of the masses
    through every conceivable medium by clever manipulation
    or subtle soft-sell appears to be more of an obstacle
    than it is a challenge and opportunity
    for bringing people into the kingdom of God.

Now I am often depressed and discouraged.
I feel at times that God has given up on me,
    that while I am a child of His grace I have failed
    to meet His demands for servanthood,
    to effectively carry out His purposes
    in stemming the tide of wickedness overwhelming
        my world,
    to proclaim and to demonstrate His redeeming love
    to people about me.
Yet I know, deep within me, that His love for me
    never ceases, that when my faith falters,
    He is ever faithful.

I must remember daily that He cares for me,
   that He is with me, that He will never let me go.
The world is in His hands, and
   despite the persistent rebelliousness of its creatures,
   He will accomplish His purposes within it.
It is not important that I see the results of my
         servanthood;
   it is important that I trust God
   and His Spirit within me—
   and that I wait quietly and patiently
   for the revealing of His kingdom.
So let come what may—adversity or affliction,
   enmity or opposition,
   feelings of defeat or even the ridicule of my peers,
   I am the redeemed child and chosen servant of my God,
   and I am His forever.

Ezekiel 2 and 3

The old preacher dozed off with his head on his desk.
He had been working on his Sunday sermon—
    trying to push off the heaviness and weariness
    encompassing him and wondering why he expected
    his congregation to stay awake during his preaching
    if he couldn't keep alert during his preparation.
These casual naps were becoming commonplace;
    only this time it was a deep sleep
    that he submitted to—one that brought on a dream
    that he wouldn't soon forget.
What he could remember about the visual aspects
    of the dream had to do with a great cloud
    and flashes of lightning and a strange,
    eerie radiance that filled the room about him.
But what he remembered best
    was the gentle but piercing voice that,
    accompanied by rumblings of thunder,
    spoke directly to him with authority and power.
It was the voice of God,
    and so the preacher listened
    with awe and some apprehension.
"You are My son, Ezekiel, and you have served Me well
    in your years upon the earth.
You have declared My love for My children.
Some have refused to hear your words
    or submit to the power of My Spirit through you;
    there are others who listened and acknowledged
    My redeeming love and are living and working
    in obedience to My will for them.

You have felt something of My grief over the rebellious
    and My joy over those who respond to My Word.
I have been with you and will continue to be with you
    in your remaining years upon the earth.
You will fearlessly proclaim My Word of judgment and
        grace
    without concern for the consequences to yourself.
Those who will not listen to you
    are those who will not listen to Me,
    and they will seek out leaders who will solace
    and comfort them in their selfishness.
You will discern their folly
    and diagnose their superficiality.
You will challenge them to face up
    to what it means to trust Me
    and to walk in obedience to My Word and will.
Listen well, Ezekiel, for I have chosen you
    to speak for Me in your community.
I will soon gather together My kingdom throughout
    your world.
There are many within hearing of My voice through you
    who are not yet a part of My kingdom.
They delude themselves into believing
    that they are My children and servants;
    they make their confessions and professions
    and assume that their religious exercises
    are accepted by Me;
    they have not, however, put aside their materialistic
        idols
    and committed themselves to My purposes.
They seek to use Me to dispense upon them comfort
    and good fortune and some guarantee of immortality,
    but they will not allow Me to use them
    in revealing and demonstrating My redeeming love
    among the peoples of the world.

They continue to live to and for themselves.
While I have borne the cross for them
    and through My suffering have set them free from
        sin's bondage,
    their response to My grace has not resulted
    in their taking up the cross on behalf of others.
Their religion is an intensely selfish,
    self-gratifying and self-glorifying activity,
    and regardless of the slogans they adopt
    and the convictions they subscribe to,
    they are in dire danger of being excluded
    from My kingdom.
Even as you proclaim my eternal love, Ezekiel,
    you must warn those who persist in making light of it,
    those who refuse to respond to it,
    those who continue to live respectable lives
    but who are not responsible in respect to My will
    and purposes for their lives."

Ezekiel 11

"Be of good cheer, old preacher," said the voice
    within his dream.
"While there are many of your peers—
    even within your congregation—who are faithless
    and disobedient, all is not lost.
It is true that some who once worshiped in sincerity
    have strayed from My fold, and others call on Me
    only to deliver them from problems and difficulties
        in their lives;
    yet I have not given up on them.
And I do not lay their faithlessness to your charge.
If their actions and activities grieve you,
    they are far more grievous to Me
    for they are My children who are going astray.
I cannot force them to return to Me, nor can you.
I will, however, even through
    your faithful proclamation of My love and grace,
    or through others whose paths they cross,
    continue to woo them back to Myself.
Some of them, after they discover the emptiness
    and loneliness of life apart from Me—
    that the world about them cannot grant the joy
    and fulfillment they once found in Me—
    will return to Me.
When they do, I shall purge them of evil
    and forgive them their sins
    and put My Spirit within them;
    and they shall be My faithful children and servants
        once more.

Nevertheless, there are those whom I will not succeed
    in drawing back to Myself
    because they will not listen to your proclamations
    or yield to the power of My Spirit.
Be faithful in your ministry, Ezekiel,
    and even while you grieve over those
    who will not respond to My saving love,
    be joyful in knowing that I am God
    and My kingdom is being advanced and served in
    and through your life and witness."

Ezekiel 16

"In your preaching, Ezekiel, remind those
    who will listen about My graciousness,
    about how much I have loved them and how patiently
    I have dealt with them throughout the years.
Most of them were committed to Me
    and were taught about Me from the time
    they were infants.
Many of them, enlightened by the study of My Word,
    consciously and zealously embraced Me as their Savior
        and Lord.
They understood something about the depths of My love
    and responded with joyous declarations of loyalty
    to Me and My purposes and were determined to follow Me
    whatever the consequences to their lives.
Some of them remained true to these declarations
    and decisions.
Others, so many others, were soon to compromise them,
    and even those who remained within religious circles
    began to tone down My claim upon their lives
    and confine Me and My Word to some small,
    Sunday-morning corner in their hearts.
They used My gifts and talents
    for their own benefit alone.
Other goals and objectives superseded My Word and will
    for these people, and they began to follow
    other shepherds into strange, foreign cults
    which promised them religious feelings without the
        necessity
    of cross-carrying and suffering.

Even some of those who stayed within the church
    sought to make My Word conform to their concoctions
    of Christianity and have, as a consequence,
    become obstacles to the advancement of My kingdom
    and purposes in your world.
There are churches in your world,
    and some people within all your churches,
    who are unwittingly ignoring My Word
    and obstructing My purposes and who are in danger
    of coming under My judgment.
Preach to them, Ezekiel.
If they refuse to hear you,
    then they are not listening to Me
    and they will not follow Me
    and I can no longer be their Savior and Lord."

Ezekiel 34

The Lord continued to speak to Ezekiel:
"Even some of My servants whom I have called
    to teach and guide My people in My ways,
    to instruct them in My Word
    and help them to discover My will and purposes,
    have been unfaithful to Me.
Some of them are ministers in large churches
    and the shepherds of huge flocks
    but are' more concerned about
    their own popularity and privileges than they are
    about recruiting and training disciples for Me.
Whereas there are scores of My children who are
    not able to sense My touch of love and comfort,
    to receive My healing power—
    and this at times because of their pastor's
        insensitivity
    to their real needs and his incapability
    of relating Me to them—
    there are others who abide in the false comfort
    of a materialistic religion
    and seek out those spiritual leaders
    who condone or encourage their style and status.
There are pastors who are feeding their own egos
    rather than the bodies and spirits of those
    for whom they have been made responsible.
These leaders are as lost
    as are the people they presume to serve,
    and they, if they do not renew their faith
    and walk in obedience to My Word,

will take upon themselves an even greater judgment
than that which falls upon their followers.
I will yet seek out the lost and wandering
whose hearts will be open to My love
and who will serve Me and My creatures
in love.
They shall hear other prophets and proclaimers
of My Word and shall be reconciled to Me.
They shall feel My touch of love and healing
through the lives of My faithful servants
from a multitude of congregations
who have become My beloved children
and who serve Me as My obedient disciples."

Ezekiel 37

Then Ezekiel, in this fabulous dream,
>was transported to a large church in some distant city.
The sanctuary was filled with worshipers—
>scrubbed-faced children and their well-dressed parents
>sat stiff and circumspect in long, mahogany pews.
The great organ was droning out Beethoven's
>"Ode to Joy" as if it were a funeral dirge while
>properly trained acolytes lit the altar candles.
The prelude concluded, the introductory strains of
>"Praise to the Lord, the Almighty" sounded forth,
>and the worshipers began mechanically mouthing
>the great words of praise and celebration
>as if they were programmed to do so.
A pastor, probably an associate or assistant,
>took charge of the liturgy
>and the congregation properly responded
>in the right places.
The beautiful words of the "Gloria in Excelsis"
>were almost totally obscured
>as a portion of the congregation dutifully stumbled
>through its musical setting.
The lessons were read by lectors, glorious words
>that should have deeply stirred the listeners,
>but sounding something like a bad tape recording
>of a dull lecture.

It was at this point that Ezekiel heard once more
>the voice of the Lord—
>as it came to the dreaming Ezekiel:

"This is where you come in, Ezekiel.
You are the preacher for the day.
Your audience is obviously uninspired and uninspiring—
    probably wishing they had stayed home
    or are thinking about the afternoon agenda
    for their lives.
Preach to these 'dead bones', Ezekiel,
    reveal to them My love and proclaim to them My Word,
    the message of My amazing grace."
And Ezekiel preached—O how he preached!
The Spirit of God kindled anew
    a fire in his old tired bones and he found himself
    joyously, enthusiastically, forcefully proclaiming
    the blessed Word of God's love for these people
        before Him.
He preached with utter abandon—
    not caring where the chips might fly
    or what his audience might think
    about what he had to say.
"You were made for God," he said,
    "and you will not discover real life or living
    apart from a loving relationship to Him.
He has come to you through Christ to touch you
    with His redeeming love, to forgive your sins,
    to set you free from the tentacles of spiritual death,
    and to make you live again—
    redeemed, reconciled to your Creator,
    restored to His will and purposes for your lives.
Then you will really be alive once more,
    and you will live and serve in joy."
He had said these things—and many other things—
    hundreds of times before to various congregations,
    but he had received what he expected—
    little if any visible response to his preaching.
This time, in his dream, it was different.

The people stirred, the sleeping awakened;
    even the noisy children quieted down,
    and the ushers leaning against the rear pillars
    stood straight and startled.
It was as if they had heard God Himself
    speaking to them through this man Ezekiel.
The organ suddenly broke excitedly and joyfully
    into a hymn of praise—
    the same hymn that opened the service—
    but this time with resurrection power,
    and the congregation rose to its feet
    and almost raised the rafters with a chorus of praise
    which was like nothing Ezekiel had ever heard before.

It was beyond Ezekiel's understanding;
    he simply could not comprehend this—
    except that it must be a dream.
Then the voice of the Lord came to him again:
    "My Spirit has spoken through you before, Ezekiel,
    and you never saw this happen in your ministry.
This is, however,
    what could happen and what will happen
    when the people to whom you preach
    will open their hearts and lives
    to the power of My Spirit.
I have not commissioned you to raise the dead;
    I have commanded you to preach—
    patiently and faithfully—
    and to leave the rest to Me.
There is nothing that you can do
    about putting flesh on dead bones or converting
    the faithless into being My children and servants
    regardless of how charming you are
    or how skillful you are in proclaiming My Word.
This is the work of My Spirit, who works through you

and through your preaching upon the hearts of those
in every congregation who are turning toward Me.
The day is coming, Ezekiel, when all who hear My Word
and yield themselves to My loving purposes
will be gathered as My eternal kingdom.
My children and My servants forever.
Arise, My son, and help to bring it to pass.
Preach, My-voice-among-your-peers,
that those who hear My Word through you
may receive My Spirit into their hearts
and place their lives and destinies in My hands.
I will be with you always."

Thus dreamed Ezekiel,
and he awakened to pursue with joy and diligence
the preparation of his next Sunday's sermon.

Hosea 1—10

Hosea married a beautiful young lady.
He had not known her for long before their union,
    and he had heard rumors to the effect
    that she was a rather frivolous girl
    who had been in and out
    of love several times.
He thought, however, that, even if that were true,
    she was now more mature, and he assumed
    that he could meet all her needs
    and have a meaningful relationship with her.
It apparently went well with this young couple
    for several years.
Though there were difficult moments—
    including those when his wife was dissatisfied and
    depressed and the several times when she threatened
    to move out and leave him—
    Hosea genuinely and idealistically loved her
    and did everything within his power to please her.

How like the love of God for His children
    was the love of Hosea for his spouse!
God has done and continues to do everything
    He can possibly do for His beloved creatures.
Though they live in a very insecure world,
    He holds them within His embrace and promises them
    the eternal security of His loving-kindness.
As frivolous and foolish
    as His wayward creatures are at times,
    He pours out His affection upon them and tenderly

speaks to them about a coming day
when they shall fully know and experience
    His infinite love,
when all their conflicts will be dissolved,
their hurts healed, their sorrows washed away,
and the deepest longings of their hearts
met and satisfied forever.
In that great day they shall know without doubt
    that God is their God and they are His children.

The wife of Hosea, however, was unwilling or incapable
of returning his love, and she eventually left him
to become involved in shallow, promiscuous
relationships with other men.
Hosea was sorely grieved and he suffered much,
not only because of his need for her,
but because of her unrecognized and unmet need
for the love that only he could offer her.
He knew she could not find true happiness
in her erratic wanderings
and the pursuance of the fleeting thrills that turn sour
and unsatisfying overnight.
He continued to love her—
hoping desperately that she would come back to him—
but she did not.
Maybe she dared not—even when she despaired over
leaving behind that which was so genuine,
or maybe because her beauty was fading
and she felt that there was no way
whereby she could deserve or experience the warmth
and security of Hosea's love again.
She would not come back to him—
perhaps she could not because of the sickness
in her heart and the ugliness of her life—
so Hosea went out to seek for her.

And he found her—
    wallowing in depravity and misery—
    and he took her back to his heart and his home
        once more.
There she found that which she could never find
    along those crooked paths she had been traversing,
    the pits in which she was existing even while
        she was dying.
She found love—tender, firm, real, secure—
    the kind of love that could transform her ugliness
    into beauty again and give meaning and purpose
    to her life that was once so empty and fruitless.

How much are the creatures of God
    like the foolish, unfaithful wife of Hosea!
God created man and woman out of the love
    of His eternal Being.
He made them free creatures
    that they might receive His love and respond in love
    to His gifts of life and joy.

Many, however, turned from their loving God
    to pursue the foolish pleasures and temporal
        treasures
    within reach around them,
    even to rebel against their Creator,
    to incur God's judgment in their whoring
    after the ephemeral delights of this world
    and worshiping those less troublesome and demanding gods
    that they made for themselves.
Even then the love of their eternal God never ceased.
He allowed them to discover for themselves
    the emptiness of their lives,
    the suffering they brought upon themselves
    through their rebellion and unfaithfulness.

God knew well that, even in their despair,
  they could not find their way back to Him again.
So, in His loving mercy, He pursued them,
  suffering in Himself the judgment they incurred
  through their infidelities,
  seeking to draw them back into His forgiving heart
  and to restore them to a loving relationship
  to Himself.
Their loving God became a suffering God
  because of His great concern for His children.
He came to them as man and God;
  He shared with them their sufferings and sorrows;
  He submitted to death on the cross
  under the scourging and nails of their rebelliousness;
  He arose from the dead as Victor over sin and death
  and, as such, made it possible for them
  to be reconciled to Him forever.

Yet even in this day,
  this day in which the love of God is revealed through
    the Christ,
  His children break out of His circle of tender concern
  and suffering love to play the harlot
  with creatures and things, philosophies and
    ideologies,
  manmade religions and cults, that promise security
  or ecstasy or riches or self-satisfaction,
  but which always fail to deliver true joy
  because they are incapable of meeting
  the eternal need of God's creatures—
  the need to be reconciled to their Creator-God
  through Jesus Christ.
Masses of God's children, blind to eternal realities,
  fascinated by cheap facsimiles,
  the bright promises, the titillating invitations

of seductive temptresses about them,
lose all sense of eternal value and waste themselves
on fast-fleeting thrills or wind-blown chaff.

God has not yet given up on them.
Even while they call judgment down upon themselves,
    He is ready to forgive them.
When they stumble into the pits that await them,
    He is waiting and ready to draw them back to Himself.
God is their true and eternal love.
Some of them will realize this before it is too late
    and allow themselves to be returned
    to His will and purposes for their lives;
    others may never turn back from those paths
    that lead to everlasting destruction.
God stands ready to forgive the infidelities
    and heal the faithlessness of His children.
If only they will confront their emptiness and loneliness,
    their great need for their true and eternal Lover,
    He will restore them to a loving relationship
    with Himself and within the family
    and kingdom of God.

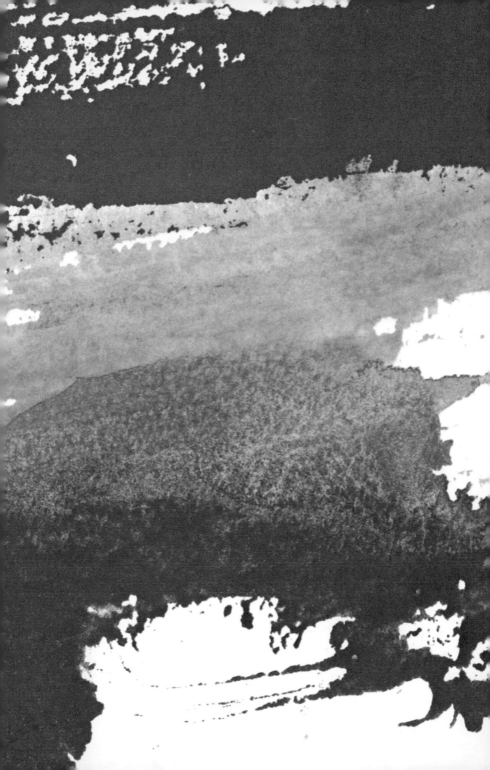

Hosea 11—14

"How profoundly I love my children
    whom I have created
    and to whom I have imparted My Spirit!"
    our great God is saying to us today.
"I continue to reveal to them My compassion;
    I help to bear their burdens and accompany them
    through the adversities that afflict them;
    I heal many of their sicknesses
    and demonstrate My loving concern
    in the midst of their deep sorrows and excruciating
        sufferings;
    I hold out to them My salvation and invite them
        to partake
    of My saving and redeeming grace.
Yet they turn from Me to pursue their own objectives.
They expend their energy upon, or seek for security
        and comfort from
    the tangible things about them—
    even those things that have come from My hand.
Even those who honor Me with their lips persist
    in dedicating their lives to the foolishness
    of the world about them.
What more can I do for My beloved children
    than I am already doing?
It is even as I love them and because I love them
    that I must allow them to go their own way,
    to satisfy their desires upon the husks of their
        temporary existence,
    to fill their emptiness with those things

that rust and decay and will pass away.
When they refuse to follow Me, I will follow them—
     even into the dark, cold caves of nothingness,
     into the pits of despair—seeking always
     to draw them back to My redeeming love,
     to restore them to My will for them.
I can do no more for My children—
     until they return to Me and commit themselves
     to My orbit for their lives."

Return, O children of God,
     to that One who created you, who loves you,
     and waits for you to come back to Him!
Repent of your folly, your sinfulness,
     you who have rebelled against your God
     and have sought for joy and peace and security
     amongst the perishable things of this world,
     and receive the eternal salvation of your God!
Cease playing god with your lives
     and return to the true God, your God
     who created and redeemed you.
He will heal the wounds caused by your faithlessness.
He will forgive and cast aside your iniquities.
Turn from your foolhardy efforts
     to pacify a righteous God with religious exercises and small
          sacrifices,
     and accept from Him the gift of life abundant
          and everlasting.
Then, and only then,
     will you bear fruit for Him,
     that as His forgiven, redeemed, and beloved children,
     you will become His chosen and empowered servants
     in your world about you.
It is then that you will know true joy and contentment
     in the discovery that He truly is your God

and He will guide you and be with you
through the hazardous days and nights of your sojourn
upon this earth.
Then you will realize what you formerly never experienced,
that the deepest longings and desires
of your inner beings are truly fulfilled—
and this even amidst the conflicts and sufferings
that plague the creatures of this planet.
God's way for you is the right way for you,
and you will live and rejoice in it,
even while the unrepentant and unbelieving around you
stumble over the paths of their own choosing.

Joel

Joel was depressed.
The conditions of the world,
    the state of the economy, the political upheavals,
    the sad tale of starving nations,
    the terrorism and torture inflicted upon vast portions
    of humanity, the rape of natural resources,
    the injustice and oppression that prey
    upon multitudes of powerless people,
    the unbridgeable gap between the rich and the poor—
    all this was finally getting to him.
And over against these apparently insurmountable problems
    was the insensitivity of his beloved church.
There was some exposure
    to community and world problems from time to time,
    and there were committees appointed to consider some
        of them,
    but bigotry, smugness, self-sufficiency,
    or a stifling sense of powerlessness,
    seemed to numb his fellow citizens
    to humanity's desperate needs
    and even turn them in upon themselves
    in their attempt to ignore them.
It was no wonder that his church was becoming
    more of a refuge for troubled Christians
    than a launching-pad for loving, sacrificial
        service—
    or that church activities centered primarily
    upon self-promoting programs designed
    to glorify the institution and enlarge the membership.

Worship was more a celebration of the people's own good
        fortune
    as the blest sons and daughters of God
    than it was of God's coming to the human family
        through Christ
    and Christ relating to the world through them.
Humanity, as they interpreted it,
    was confined to those people around them
    who belonged to their own race and culture
    and economic status.
This was a problem with most churches, as Joel saw it.
They had become sacred clubs
    rather than channels of power and healing
    to a violent, fractured world.
They couldn't even relate to one another—
    his own church and the others within his community—
    for each of them was zealously guarding its own
        precious doctrines
    and relishing its own spiritual experiences.

Joel was convinced that God was the answer to humankind's
        needs
    and had made available the power that was far greater
    than the selfishness and wickedness of the world's
        inhabitants.
He was convinced, as well, that the channels
    through which this divine power was to flow—
    the lives and experiences of God's redeemed creatures—
    were clogged up with pride, self-concern, and anxieties
    about their own material and physical welfare.
Joel was just becoming aware
    of God's expectations for his children and servants
    and how far he fell short of Christ's command
    to take up the cross and follow Him.

In his attempts to become a responsible Christian,
    he felt an ever widening gap between himself
    and his church-member friends.
Thus Joel was depressed and,
    though determined to follow Christ irrespective of
        cost or consequences,
    felt lonely and frustrated as he viewed world problems
    over against the churches that were more concerned
    about growing fat than they were
    about growing spiritually tall and strong
    and thereby becoming, under God, a force
    with which to be reckoned.
Many of his fellow Christians remained perpetually
        satisfied
    with the milk of God's saving grace
    when they should have been moving on
    toward the meat of loving discipleship.

Out of his depression
    Joel poured out his feelings before God.
God's Word came alive as he searched for answers
    to his great concern.
"I have not given up on My church in your world, My son,"
    he seemed to hear God saying.
"The institution is weak and foolish
    and full of self-concern.
It is, nevertheless, where My Spirit is at work
    and where I am finding among its many constituents
    a remnant of faithful children who will hear My Word
    and embrace My saving grace
    and become My devoted and obedient servants.
As I did not give up on you, Joel,
    but patiently led you to a deeper relationship with Me,
    so I will not, and neither should you,
    give up in regard to your church and those therein

who will give their lives to My service.
Take heart, my son,
    for I am doing great things in your world.
They may not always be visible to you,
    but they are happening.
My Spirit, working in your life
    and through the lives of people of your church,
    will make you and them the ministers of My grace
        and power
    that will give life to the dying, sight to the blind,
    strength to the weak, and hope and joy
    to the hopeless and unhappy people of your world.
It won't happen all at once, but this has been happening
    since the beginning of the human family,
    and will continue until My kingdom is fully revealed
    and all of My children will be delivered
    once and for all from your sin-ridden planet
    to be My sons and daughters forever.
Stop fretting, Joel,
    and begin living up to that measure of grace
    that I have imparted to you.
Love your fellow members,
    and show by your life in Me the joy and security
    that, even in the midst of many adversities,
    is available to all who will yield themselves
    to Me and My purposes.
Rejoice in Me;
    celebrate My love for you and for all My creatures;
    proclaim through your living and speaking
    My redeeming grace and loving Lordship
    and the power of My Spirit to bring healing and life
        to your world's masses
    through those who will walk in faith
    and serve their fellow persons in obedience to Me."

Amos

His name was Amos.
He lived on a small farm in a rich and powerful
      Western country.
His home was in one of the northern states of a land
    that was teeming with church structures
    and with large and small congregations
    that gathered every week to sing the praises of God
    and to hear the joy-giving proclamations
    of God's redeeming love.
He was a dairy farmer, this man named Amos,
    who had read much and felt deeply and prayed intensely
    that he might be used in some way to bring people
    into the kingdom of God.
It was his compelling desire to tell others
    about the love of God and His saving grace
    that they might know the great joy
    of being God's forgiven, redeemed, and beloved
        sons and daughters.
But he was sorely disturbed by the attitudes and
        activities
    of many Christian institutions and their constituents
    in respect to what was transpiring in the world
    and about what he considered to be unchristian
    and ungodly responses or reactions to people
    and events within the world.
One Sunday, while the regular pastor was
    on his vacation, Amos had an opportunity to preach
    in the local congregation.
He determined to air his concerns

and, instead of proclaiming the way of salvation
with the hope that his words might reach
some troubled unbeliever in the assembly,
he directed his words to his Christian brothers
        and sisters.

He began by identifying some of the concerns
        that were threatening to the life of a Christian
        and to the church and which they could all agree
        were under the judgment of God.
"We are all united
        in our condemnation of totalitarian philosophy
        and its devastating effects upon our world,"
                he said.
"There is no doubt as to where the church stands
        in respect to the evils such as pornography
        and sexual promiscuity that are infiltrating our
                community
        and corrupting our youth.
We proclaim God's judgment upon all the false religions
        that are being propagated throughout our country—
        even those off-shoot cults that seduce our youth
        into making commitments contrary to the faith
        that we approve of and to the religious activities
        in which we half-heartedly participate.
We applaud our government in its endeavors
        to protect our culture and sustain our security
        and guarantee our freedom to own property
        and accumulate wealth.
It seldom occurs to us, however,
        that we who fly the Christian banner
        are often worshiping the gifts that God has
                given us
        rather than our heavenly Father—
        and are serving our own self-interests

rather than being His servants to His creatures
about us.
While we are comparably rich
in view of this world's masses
that struggle so desperately for survival,
we refuse to accept, or even admit, responsibility
for our careless contributions
to their deprivation and oppression.
We assume we are deserving of our good fortune
and we overindulge in food and drink and
luxurious living
as if we were the favored sons and daughters
of God.
We have been guilty of fashioning God in our own
image
and interpreting His principles in terms of our selfish
needs and wishes.
Rather than being the forerunner,
we are often the tail end
of secular movements pressuring our society
for equal rights and opportunities on behalf
of minority groups in our country.
We correlate God and human government
in such a way that it frees us from the risk
of making Christlike decisions and commitments
that may threaten our security or prosperity.
We give the allegiance that is due only God
to human and fallible leaders who expect our support
even when they have no intention
of respecting the rights and needs of the human
family.
The church has often wrapped itself
in its own self-inflating programs
that ignore the desperate needs of minority
or other-culture people in their community.

Our congregations too often become an end unto
        themselves
    with little concern for the poor and oppressed
    or for the rights of persecuted and tortured human
        beings
    in the world around them.
As churches, congregations—
    as the very sons and daughters of God—
    we are often not patterning our lives
    after the Christ whose life and salvation
        we proclaim.
Whereas our doctrines are correct
    and our worship practices inspiring,
    we have fallen far short of God's will and
        purposes
    in our practice of the Christian faith,
    and in some ways may be far more comparable
    to the Pharisees who persecuted the Christ
    than to the disciples who followed in His steps.
The truth is, even for those who claim and proclaim
        God's grace,
    His judgment begins with us, because so many of us
    are making our primary commitment
    to things other than God and His will for our lives.

Among the churches of our great country
    there is a remnant—those faithful servants of God
    in every congregation—who are discovering what it means
    to follow Jesus Christ.
They are blessed indeed.
They are willing to risk all—
    prosperity, material security, jobs, reputations,
        even their lives—
    to be like Christ and to channel the healing,
    saving power of Christ to people about them.

The church at large, though under judgment,
        is the institution out of which these come forth;
        and because of these who truly love God
        and become the vehicles of His love,
        others will repent of their self-centeredness
        and apathy and recognize anew the pain and joy
        of genuine discipleship.
They are those who really live,
        abundantly and joyfully, as they faithfully
        and obediently worship and serve their God
        in the process of serving God's creatures
                about them."

Thus preached Amos on that Sunday morning
        in his hometown church.
The congregation listened.
Some even expressed appreciation for his fine message.
They returned to their homes and farms to eat,
        sleep, work—exist—as they had done
        all their lives.
Most of them would be back in their respective pews
        next Sunday morning.

Jonah

There was a pastor named Jonah
    who was comfortably and happily involved
    with a little congregation in a rural-type town
    in a Midwestern state.
He loved his parishioners and they loved him,
    and he expected to serve this little group
    of faithful Christians for years to come.
One day he received a Letter of Call
    from the Board of World Missions of his denomination.
He was requested to consider an assignment
    as missionary to a large city in Central Asia.
He was honored, of course,
    and there was something strangely compelling
    about this invitation—as if the Lord Himself
    had sent it and was speaking to him through it—
    but Jonah had no inclination toward foreign-mission
        service
    and so promptly returned the Letter of Call
    with the explanation that he had found his niche
    as a Christian pastor and had no intention of
        leaving it.

It was soon after this, as Jonah tells it,
    that things seemed to go wrong with his life.
He no longer felt as happy or comfortable
    with his work in his parish.
He wondered if he may have been careless
    in so quickly refusing the Board of World Mission's
        invitation,

and he was plagued by occasional bouts of deep
       depression
which he could not easily cast off.
It became worse in the ensuing weeks,
       and he was forced to face up to God
       concerning the disturbing unrest of his soul.
He prayed as he had never prayed before:
       "I feel as if I have dried up, O Lord,
       almost as if Your Spirit has left me.
I no longer am so sure that I belong here,
       and insurmountable obstacles seem to have
       come between me and my people.
I no longer sense the joy I used to feel
       over my work in this place, only heaviness
       and discouragement, as if I were lost in some dark
           night
       or slowly suffocating under some unbearable
           pressure.
I am ready, my God,
       if Your plans for me lead elsewhere,
       to go where You would have me go
       and do what You want me to do."
He prayed it—and he honestly meant it.
Though he received no sure response to his pleading,
       he gave thanks to God for the assurance
       that his prayer was heard,
       that God was merciful and would be with him
       in the midst of this conflict in his life.

Just one week later he received another letter
       from the Board of World Missions
       repeating the invitation to foreign service
       and urging him to reconsider.
This time Jonah was convinced
       that God was speaking to him through that letter.

The moment he dispatched his response
    informing the Board of his decision to accept the
        appointment,
    he was totally released from the stifling spirit
    of oppression that hovered in and about him;
    and he was at peace with God.

One month later he left his little parish
    for that strange, foreboding new world
    to which he was assigned.
He was filled with apprehension,
    but he knew that he had been sent by God
    and that God was with him all the way.
There were many difficulties to overcome in that
    Central Asian city, such as language, culture-shock,
    loneliness, even a daily feeling of insecurity
    among these people so different from his own kind
    that he had worked with in his former parish;
    but he eventually learned how to communicate
    with them—and to love them—and found them
    surprisingly receptive to the Gospel of Jesus Christ.
The whole city did not bow down to Christ
    as did the city of Nineveh in the days
    of that Jonah who preached to them,
    but a beginning was made; Christians were
        recruited,
    and God's purposes were being carried out
        in that place.

Jonah learned afresh two great truths.
One was the necessity of obedience to the call
    of the Spirit of God, and that, as God's servant,
    he was constantly under orders and must be ready
    to follow them wherever they may lead him.
The second great truth is that God's eternal presence

circumscribes the whole world and includes all its
    peoples,
and His Spirit is preparing hearts
for the proclamation of His saving grace and
is searching out those men and women
who will make that proclamation.

Micah

Micah was the spiritual leader
    of a small congregation in the hill country.
His people were very poor, and Micah himself
    subsisted on the labors of his own hands
    and occasional love-gifts brought to him
    by his beloved parishioners.
He was a vigorous man—
    and a man with insight and wisdom.
He could have left his village
    and done better for himself
    in some wealthier, more populous area,
    but, partly because of his concern
    for the poor and deprived about him
    and because of his smoldering anger
    toward those institutions and leaders
    that were directly or indirectly responsible
        for his people's poverty,
    he stayed with his people to comfort them
    even while he poured out God's words of judgment
    upon nations and rulers, including
    even middle-class church leaders and church members,
    who smugly carried on their activities
    with little or no regard for the indigent
    and the oppressed.

"The day is coming," said Micah,
    "when our great God will make Himself known
    to the world and its peoples and will even up
        the score.

He will expose corruption and root out
    the dark activities of selfish leaders.
Even our own nation, and the institutions and
        corporations
    that have contributed to its depravation
    will not escape the judgment
    of our almighty God.
Nor will its constituents who have dedicated themselves
    to material wealth and comfort
    with no thought whatever about what happens
    to the impoverished and powerless people about them
    escape this divine judgment.
Those who consider themselves singled out
    and so richly blessed by God
    in the hoard of worldly treasures about them will
        discover
    that God's primary concern is for the very masses
    they despise or consider their inferiors.
Manmade standards shall be exploded,
    earthbound values superseded;
    success and significance shall be ascertained
    by a higher power than the finite, foolish
    minds of this world.
How will God break up this power block
    that secures the rich and discomfits the poor,
    or distribute the wealth that enriches the few
    and impoverishes the masses of this world's
        inhabitants?
It has happened in the past;
    it may happen again—some terrible catastrophe
    or an invading enemy may be allowed by God
    to perpetrate its mischief while perpetuating
        His judgments.
But happen it will—
    whatever the means and in God's own time—

and the powerful and oppressive who have grown fat
on this world's treasures will be unable to deter it."

Micah may not always have been fair with the
        politicians,
    and he should have recognized
    that some of them were concerned about people
    and motivated by benign intent,
    but he generally lumped them all together
    and flayed them unmercifully
    before his listeners.
"They are more concerned about high salaries
    for themselves than they are people's problems
    even while they squeeze the populace with taxes
    in order to secure their own future.
They spend huge amounts to insure and protect
    their high standard of living
    while allowing a pittance to raise
    the standard of living for the poor.
They promote a system of justice
    that favors the rich and influential
    while it fails to protect the powerless people
    in our society.
They, themselves, will be begging for justice someday,"
    said Micah, "but they may not obtain it in that day
    when their selfish activities will be exposed
    for all the world to see."

Then Micah took on the spiritual leaders of nation
        and world,
    particularly those with large churches
    filled with well-to-do people
    whose religious beliefs and activities appeared
    to have little effect on the community-
        at-large.

"They pour out platitudes
when they should be proclaiming the judgment of God
upon the kind of worship and religious activities
that result in making people numb to the horrendous
sufferings
that afflict the masses of our world.
They work to keep their constituents happy
and at peace with one another
when they should be declaring war against
any attempt or tendency to dilute or compromise
God's blessed Word into a pacifying rather than
a provoking Gospel.
They judge their success and effectiveness
by the huge shrines they build
and the large numbers of people that fill them.
They package religion into a respectable,
inoffensive, law-abiding, good-works format
that promises their adherents
the feeling of being religious
without demanding any changes
in their lives and activities.
They avidly proclaim
God's acceptance of people as they are
but dare not exemplify or challenge people
in terms of allowing God to make them
what He expects them to be."

It could be expected
that Micah might have been a little jealous
over some of his success-oriented colleagues
who were making their mark in his generation,
but he was sincerely concerned about how little
the mammoth religious organizations of his country
that, claiming to promote the Gospel of God's love
and saving grace as revealed through Jesus Christ,

were able to draw people to this Christ
        as the Scriptures revealed Him
        and challenging them to follow Him.
Micah was aware, of course,
        that there were scores of faithful pastors
        and church people throughout the land;
        but it seemed to him that the church institution,
        in many instances, was the enemy of God—
        an obstacle to the accomplishment of His purposes
        and the advancement of His kingdom
        throughout the world.
God will judge—He does judge—the world's institutions,
        political, commercial, educational, religious,
        that knowingly or unwittingly are leading people astray.
He doesn't stop there, however,
        for according to Micah, ultimate judgment
        falls upon the people themselves.
It is people who make up nations and institutions;
        it is people who must inevitably face up
                to the true God.
And it is these people who seek their own personal
                welfare
        and whose self-seeking and luxurious living
        perpetrate injustice and oppression and deprivation
        upon humankind about them.
They create their own gods or religions
        that condone their avaricious activities,
        and many of these people are foolish enough
        to call such Christianity.

"There is still hope," proclaimed Micah.
"There is a remnant scattered throughout the land.
It consists of those who are learning what it means
        to follow Jesus Christ.
They have not only embraced the righteousness of God

as revealed through His Son,
but they have responded to His gift of grace
in dedicating their lives to His purposes.
And His purposes, they are discovering, lead them
to forsake self-seeking and luxurious living
and to enlist in His mission
of communicating His love and saving power
to their brothers and sisters in the human family.
Such a course will be threatening
to their national security—
even their reputations, their social status—
if not their very lives.
It is the course Jesus took before them
and which for Him involved suffering and struggle
and death on a cross.
It means putting the concerns and needs of others
even above one's own.
It is the course, however,
that leads to genuine fulfillment in this life
and everlasting joy and contentment in the life
and kingdom of God,
which is soon to be fully revealed."

This was the message of Micah.
He would not have been very popular in a large,
wealthy parish in the metropolis,
but the Spirit of God was speaking through him
in that little congregation in the hill country.

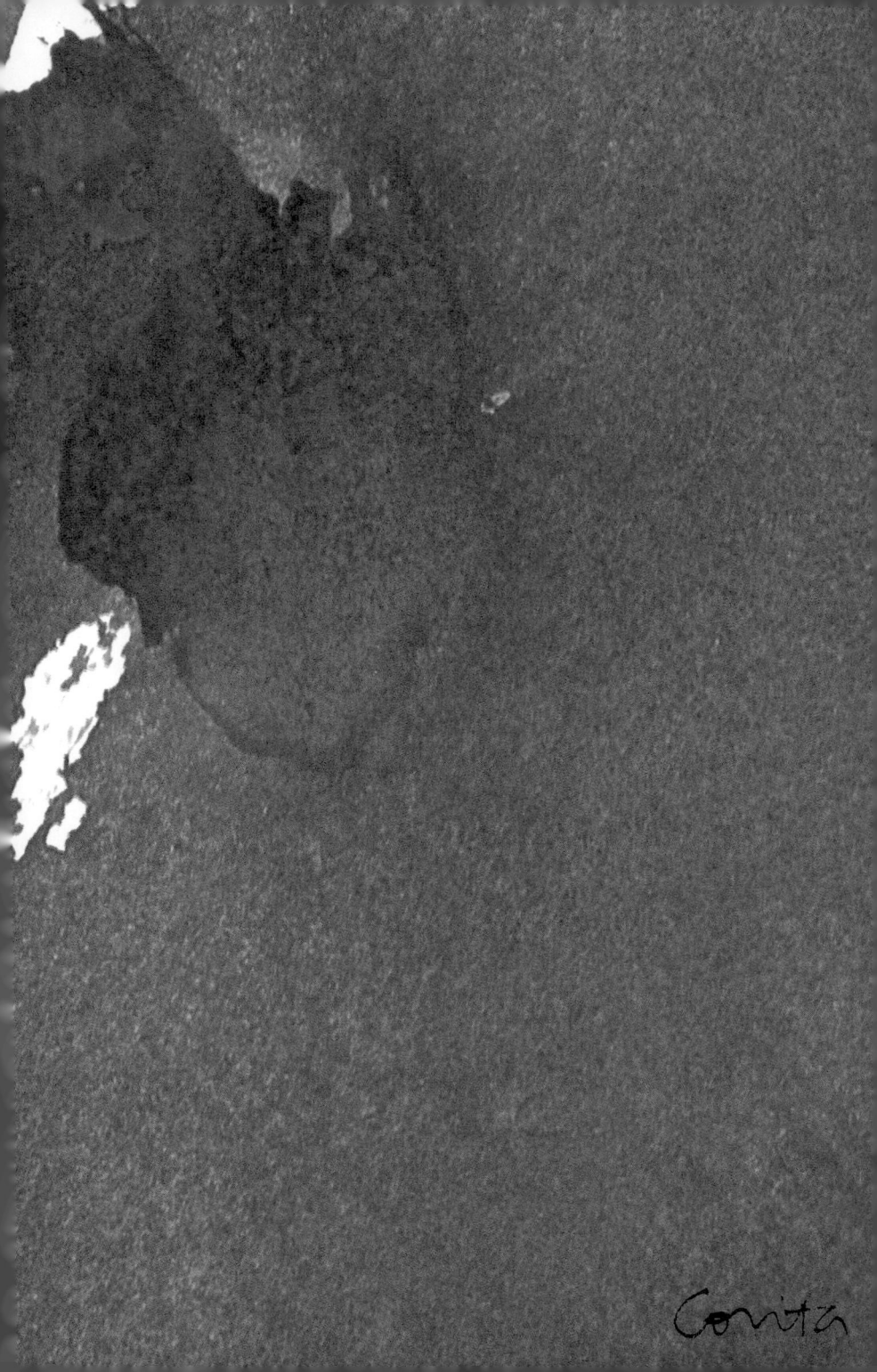

Corita

Habakkuk

O God, how long must I wait for Your intervention
    in this sorry world You have created?
Things have gone awry; wickedness reigns supreme.
Lawlessness and injustice are rampant all about me.
There is violence and destruction wherever I turn.
Whatever is good and right is being stifled by
    evil and error.
Morning, noon, and night
    I am bombarded with trouble,
    immersed in strife,
    plagued by contention and conflict.

"Have courage, My child.
You see with your eyes and hear with your ears
    the sights and sounds about you.
Can you not perceive in your heart
    that I am still Lord and God
    over all the earth?
Are you not allowing the whirlwind and the thunder
    to dull your spiritual sensitivities?
Do you dare to imagine
    that the noisy games that people play
    are capable of blanking out My will
    and purposes for your world?
Be calmed, and allow My Spirit within you
    to interpret to you what is transpiring
    behind the scenes.
Look to what is happening through My eyes
    and see what I am doing among the nations

and peoples of your world.
Is it so amazing to you that even the wickedness
and rebelliousness of My creatures are working
toward the accomplishment of My purposes?"

I know, O God,
that You are from everlasting to everlasting.
You are holy and righteous
and cannot condone the evils and wrongdoings
of Your earthly creatures.
Then why, O Lord, do You appear
to be so indifferent to the sufferings
of Your faithful children?
Why do You allow them
to be oppressed and swallowed up by selfish,
abusive people about them?
These poor creatures don't know where to turn,
or where they might seek for help.
They are powerless, leaderless,
ready prey for the beasts that mill round them
or the clever foxes that seek to take advantage
over them.
Is there not some way
in which You can stop the bloodletting,
the starving, the persecuting, the violence
being inflicted upon the bodies and spirits
of your beloved children within this world?

"Stop complaining, My servant.
This is the world to which I entrusted you and
all My children.
It is wracked by evil and shadowed by darkness
and filled with violence and injustice.
You are to be patient—and to be faithful to Me—

amidst your suffering world and your numerous
    unresolved questions.
It is out of your world that I shall redeem
    and purge and make righteous a remnant
    who will be reconciled to Me and will become
    My everlasting kingdom.
That time will come soon enough.
You are, in the meantime, to trust in Me,
    to follow Me in faith, to wait in patience,
    to serve in love as are all My sons and
        daughters in your world.
As to the faithless, the arrogant and rebellious,
    the irredeemable sons and daughters of darkness,
        never fear;
    for they shall receive their just due."

I have heard God speaking and my whole being quivers
    with a strange fusion of awe and joy.
I sense anew the miracle God has wrought
    in my redemption.
I am determined to wait upon my God,
    to trust in His infinite wisdom.
Even in this day of trouble and conflict I will wait—
    and I will serve.
While falsehood appears to be mightier than the truth
    and darkness seems to blot out the sun
    and evil to overcome righteousness,
        I will wait and serve my loving, almighty, eternal God.
In Him I will rejoice;
    for He is the God of my salvation.
He is my Joy and Strength and will keep me
    and all of His faithful children and servants
    in the midst of the storms that batter against us.

Zephaniah

Zephaniah was a deacon at First Church in South City.
He was a gloomy sort of fellow, inclined to see
   the dark side of most things and not a bit hesitant
   about pointing it out to anyone who would listen
      to him.
At least that is what his casual friends noted
   about this man.
Those who were closest to him, however,
   learned to respect his opinions,
   and recognized that he was a profoundly religious man
   with insights that were as rich and rare
   as ancient wine.
He was, for one thing, very disturbed about the state
   of the world and, particularly, his own country.
He loved his country and had little use
   for those people who were constantly putting it down.
On the other hand,
   he would not stand for the superpatriotic concepts
   of very naive citizens who assumed that
   their nation was God's very special concern,
   a sort of "new Jerusalem"
   that would be perpetually blest by their Creator.
"Regardless of the reference to God
   in the Constitution and the 'In God We Trust' slogan
   on the nation's hard currency—
   which is in itself little short of blasphemy—
   our country is under the judgment of God,"
   Zephaniah was quick to say.
He doubted very much

that God was any more pleased with his nation
than He was with the less esteemed countries
of the world.
This may have been one reason
for Zephaniah's perennial gloom.
While he noted with appreciation those national leaders
who appeared to have a genuine religious faith,
he was suspicious even of them and their real motives.
It happened too often that those
who made numerous references to the Deity
were often the very ones who made or supported
decisions
that were favorable to their private interests.
The corruption in high places appalled Zephaniah.
"How can leaders claim they are following God's will
even while they lead their constituents
into some destructive war on foreign soil
or vote for measures that favor the rich over
against the poor
or who deliberately obstruct justice
in their attempts to protect themselves
and their personal concerns," said Zephaniah.
It was not only the leaders of his country's
government that angered him,
but the activities of local leaders and politicians—
some of whom he knew—that deepened his pessimism.
Even many of those who had the most altruistic ideals
when they took over their offices
often forgot all about those goals
after their entrenchment in leadership positions.
A couple of them even belonged to his own church
and appeared to be devout and respectable
on Sundays, only to carry on some very unchristian
activities
back in their offices on Monday.

First Church in South City had an excellent pastor,
  and Zephaniah was pleased with the number of people
     within the congregation
  who appeared to be genuinely Christian
  and were obviously growing in their understanding
  of God's will for their lives.
He was very disturbed, however, about the larger number
  of church members who were just skirting the edge
  of the Christian faith and its responsibilities.
God, or so it appeared, was a very small part
  of their daily lives and schedules.
They looked to God as a dispenser of good things
  and felt strongly that the church and its teachings
  would have a positive effect on their families
  and even their personal lives,
  but they were not about to make Christ and His
     teachings
  their primary objective and goal.
As far as Zephaniah was concerned,
  they were still children of the world hung up
  on its acquisitions and their own personal
     achievements,
  struggling for ever higher standards of living,
  and were using the church as one of the agencies
  that enabled them to discover fulfillment
  or success or security as they interpreted it
  in very temporal terms.
They nodded in assent to the proclamations of God's love
  and concern for them but were numb to anything
  beyond that—anything that might challenge
  or instruct them in respect to God and His purposes
  for their lives.
It was apparent to Zephaniah that most of this group
  were not about to take Jesus Christ seriously—
  at least not His call and command to follow Him

or to be His vehicles of loving service to humanity
about them.
They made God in their own image, these people,
and assumed they were meeting His standards
if they lived by their self-concocted rules
and questionable moralities.

Zephaniah loved his nation and, above all, his church.
Depressed at times
and very critical about contemporary Christianity
as interpreted and followed by some national
and local leaders and a great many church members,
he found himself ever striving,
sometimes painfully and often unsuccessfully,
to measure up to what he believed Jesus
had commanded and enabled him to be.
He was challenged, yet troubled, with dreams
and visions of what a truly Christian nation,
and especially a Spirit-filled church, could be
if those who professed Jesus Christ would truly live
in loving and risk-filled obedience to His Word.
Zephaniah was convinced that the nation, as such,
along with all human governments, would fall under
the judgment of God and ultimately be wiped out.
There was little doubt, in his mind, that such
would eventually happen to the institutional church.

Where Zephaniah's spirit
was raised to the heights and his optimism abounded
was in the ancient promise that God would one day
gather his faithful children out of all nations
and religious institutions to make up the new kingdom,
the eternal kingdom of God.
"That will be the day," exclaimed Zephaniah.
"It will be at the time when those who are

walking with God and faithfully serving Him—
in individual arenas of service
as well as through the church institution—
by loving and serving their fellow beings,
will share the joy and victory of their Lord forever.
That will be the day when all that is selfish
and immoral and corrupt will be cleansed from the earth
and the God of beauty and love, justice
and abundance, will reign in everlasting power
over every one of his creatures."

Zephaniah rejoiced in the vision of that day to come.
He firmly believed it would come.
It was when he withdrew his thoughts
from that ultimate scene to confront present-day
realities about him
that he tended to become a gloomy sort of fellow.

"Do not be afraid," our God would say to Zephaniah
and to each of us today.
"Let not your hearts become faint or your hands grow weak.
I am in your midst, and the final victory is Mine.
I will warm and renew your hearts with My love.
I will keep you even amidst the conflicts and
sufferings that besiege you.
I will deal severely with all that is evil.
I will deliver those who are in bondage
and heal those who are sick and bring justice
to those who have been oppressed.
And I will bring you and all My children home.
Then you shall rejoice and sing aloud and offer
your praises to your Creator-God and King."

Haggai

As God spoke in ages past through bold young prophets
   like Haggai, He speaks to us in our century
   through them and others who hear His Word
   above the tumult and tempest of people's selfish
      struggles
   for self-gain and self-fulfillment.
As God's chosen people of Haggai's time virtually
   ignored God's purposes and utilized His gifts to
   secure comfort and security for themselves,
   so those He has appointed for His purposes and
   objectives in this generation are investing their
   God-given talents and opportunities in their personal
   comfort and security—ignoring not only God's will
   and plan for their lives, but making little effort
   and no sacrifice whatever
   to share their abundance with the deprived
   and oppressed masses that mill about them
   in their world.
We call ourselves God's children;
   but when the score is added up, we may discover
   that we are rebellious children,
   disobedient children who have fallen
   out of God's plan for our lives and are
   separated from His saving grace.
We know that God redeems us
   and grants us His forgiving love,
   that He took upon Himself
   His judgment upon our faithlessness that we may be
      restored to Him.

But if we do not respond to His gift of salvation
    and dedicate our lives to His purposes,
    how dare we continue to call ourselves His children?
No matter how enthusiastic our proclamations of faith,
    if our lives do not increasingly reveal the same
    through the working of His Spirit in and through us—
    and this in our relationships to our fellow persons—
    then something is frightfully wrong with our faith
    and our relationship to our loving God.

"When you return to Me, you return to My will
    for your lives," our God would say to us.
"It is not possible for you to continue living
    and building and investing solely for yourselves
    and your small circle of loved ones
    while multitudes of My creatures are hungry
    and oppressed, and yet continue to remain
    My children and servants.
My will and purposes for you
    are not centered within, nor confined to, your
        little plot of land
    or even to your church up the block;
    they include the world and all its inhabitants.
You are, as My children,
    assigned to be the instruments through which My Spirit
    can work within your world.
When you ignore My purposes,
    you become an obstacle rather than a vessel,
    and you are abandoning Me and My will for you."

"I entreat you," says our God,
    "to consider your foolish, selfish investments,
    to recognize how unfulfilling and empty they are.
You have had a taste of better things;

you will no longer be satisfied with anything less
than My will for you.
Allow My Spirit to have his way with you—
to lead you to the joy of enlisting in My purposes.
There will be pain—I never promised anything less.
There will be sacrifice—this is the price of true love.
There will be failures and disappointments—
you will grieve as I grieve over those who will not
come to Me.
There is, nonetheless, joy abundant, fulfilling—
for such is My gift to those who follow Me
and who commit themselves to My will and purposes
in your world.
And there is My guarantee
that I will always be with you—
encouraging, strengthening, forgiving,
loving, enabling—and the life you live
in the center of My will is far better
than anything you can garner or gain
for yourself, and it will be forever."

Malachi

"I love My people whom I have created
  and for whom I have suffered
  that they may be set free from sin's bondage
  and serve Me as My children and servants."
God was speaking to Malachi,
  a young, ambitious preacher who was called
  to occupy the pulpit of a large, prestigious church
    in Central City.
He had proclaimed joyfully God's love
  to his parishioners, and they had responded
  with generous gifts that had finally paid off the
    property debt
  on their beautiful sanctuary.
Now, however, or so it seemed, the congregation
  had reached the pinnacle of success
  and an atmosphere of apathy was settling
  upon them like a dark cloud.
It disturbed and depressed young Malachi
  as he strode up and down the aisles
  of his empty church one Tuesday morning.
This was the time of prayer—getting his head and heart
  together before tackling the week's duties before him.
It was at this time that he was most sensitive to the
  voice of God's Spirit within him.
He had often heard God speak to him through His Word
  and Spirit concerning His great love for His children,
  but Malachi seemed to hear other things this morning.
"I love My people—but I am deeply grieved
  over the way they respond to My love."

Maybe Malachi was arguing with himself,
    but he blurted out aloud,
        "Why, Lord, are You grieved?
Behold the beautiful sanctuary built to glorify You.
Look at the expensive stained windows that portray
    Your redeeming love in picture and symbol.
Listen to our great organ that fills our place of worship
    with hymns of praise, our carillon chimes
        that peal out the message of Your love to our neighborhood
            about us."
"I see and hear all these things,
    but they do not bring joy to My heart," Malachi
    heard the Spirit say within him.
"I expect far more from My children
    than their small sacrifices on your church altar
    or their feeble attempts to enlarge your
        church rolls."
"What more do You expect from us?" agonized Malachi.
"How can we respond to Your everlasting love?"
"The offerings you bring to your altar
    may build buildings and beautify sanctuaries
    and make more comfortable and inspiring the place
    in which you sing and pray and listen to
        My Word,"
    said the Spirit of God,
        "but they are unacceptable to Me.
I cannot bless them or glory in them
    because they are not love-offerings.
They are but a pittance designed to solace Me
    when I am waiting for the kind of love and loyalty
    that will result in serving Me."
"We assumed that we had been serving you, O God,"
    prayed Malachi, "What can we do?"
"You must continue to proclaim My love even while
    making My people aware of their responsibilities

as My children and My servants," said the Spirit.
"What kind of offerings are acceptable to You?"
    inquired Malachi.
"The whole offering, the total offering,
    of your very minds and bodies dedicated to
    and perpetually involved in My objectives
    and purposes in your world.
You need not ask me how these offerings are to be made.
I have already sent you My Son to reveal that to you.
He will come again and will judge as to whether or not
    My children have lovingly responded
    to His example
        and injunctions.
I can assure you that if He came today,
    He would find many who worship in your sanctuary
    to be unfaithful and disobedient.
They have sought for Me only to use Me with little
    intention of allowing Me to use them.
They have used their sanctuary as a place of refuge
    from the world's problems rather than a supply station
    for service to My creatures throughout your world,
    and they are shielding themselves from the sufferings
    and injustices heaped upon their fellow beings
    about them rather than becoming My servants
    lovingly involved in bringing My comfort and healing
    and saving grace to those in need.
Can you not see it, Malachi?
There are all kinds of respectable God-worshipers
    who build churches and sing My praises,
    but who are, in effect, embezzlers, swindlers,
    liars, and cheaters, in their relationship to Me.
You may have been faithful in proclaiming My love,
    but have you been faithful
    in announcing My expectations concerning those
    whom I love and reconcile to Myself?

And are you, yourself,
        setting the example in your own life,
        or are you in danger of becoming ensconced
        in that warm, little nest
        you have helped to create?
The day is coming when your beautiful buildings
        will crumble and become like the dust of the earth,
        when all your remarkable programs and ego-satisfying
        statistics will be scattered like leaves in the wind.
That which remains will be
        that which has served to channel My love
        to the peoples of your community and world—
        that which is accomplished only through the loving
            sacrifices of My servants
        who have truly responded to My love
        by committing their lives to My service.
There is still time, Malachi,
        for you and your parishioners to bring
        acceptable sacrifices to My altar,
        to offer your sacrifices on the altar
        of your neighbor's needs,
        to allow Me through you to recruit servants
        who will honor Me and walk in obedience to My will
        for their lives and become My instruments,
        My vessels of love and power
        assigned to seek out and save the suffering,
        oppressed, lonely, and lost people about them.
Then I will bless your labors and accept your praises,
        for the members of your congregation will be responding
        to My love by lovingly relating to each other's needs
        as well as the needs of reachable people around them."

John, Revelation 2 and 3

The Church at Ephesus:

Your congregation, from its very inception,
    has been a hard-working congregation.
You have held firm to the faith amidst numerous
       adversities.
Your pastors have been strong, doctrinally sound leaders
     who have led you deeply into the Word
     and have implanted within you a genuine appreciation
     for the theology of the church.
You have reflected this in your life and worship together.
Yet something is sadly missing in your fellowship.
While you have been correct in discerning false
       teachings
     and in avoiding those who peddle them,
     something equally insidious has crept in among you.
You are apparently more concerned
     about the letter of the Law than the spirit
       of the Gospel;
       you are becoming dogmatic—even arrogant—
     in your insistence that you are the possessors of
       exact truth
     and therefore will have nothing to do with people
     who have somewhat diverse ideas about God
     and His Word for the world today.
This attitude may have shielded you from false doctrines
     and kept your teachings properly orthodox,
     but it has resulted in something even more grievous.
You have not learned the most important lesson of all—

how to love your fellow beings as your sisters and
      brothers in Christ.
If your love for God as revealed through Christ
      does not resolve in the compulsion to love
      your fellow persons—irrespective of their inability
      to totally accept and abide by your precepts—
      then your love for God is in question.
Thus you are enjoined to examine yourselves,
      to recognize and repent of your lovelessness,
      and to embrace anew God's great love
      as demonstrated in Jesus Christ and then reach out
      in love to the human family about you.
It is only then that the faith you profess
      and the doctrines you so zealously protect
      and expound will become living and redemptive
      in the lives of others with whom you come in contact.

The Church at Smyrna:

Your congregation is small.
Economically, at least, your resources are very limited.
You have, at times, been infiltrated by individuals
      who have attempted to influence you with teachings
      that might have jeopardized your strong faith
      in Christ as your Savior and Lord.
You have resisted their divisive demands,
      and though a few have been stolen away
      from your assembly while others have been persecuted
      because they refused to yield to false teachings,
      most of you have held firm in your Bible-based beliefs.
You must continue in that worthy determination,
      knowing that what you might lose in doing this

is of small value when compared with losing
your faith in Jesus Christ.

You are small, but you are potent—
      and you are important to your Lord and Christ.
Continue to be faithful to Him,
      whatever the immediate consequences;
      and you will eventually wear the crown of victory
      and know forever the joy of being, with Christ,
      the sons and daughters of God.

The Church at Pergamum:

Your congregation is to be commended—
      located as it is in the slum area of the inner city.
Your property vandalized, your very lives endangered,
      you continue to faithfully proclaim
      the Word of God's love for His creatures
      wherever they are and whatever their economic
            status or living standards.
And God's Word is being heard by those seeking souls
      who are being reached by your ministry.
There are problems, however, within your church.
There are some people, and they have some influence
      among your members, who are racist in their actions
      and a stumbling block to God's purposes for your
            congregation.
There are others who are unwittingly causing division
      among you by their insistence upon signs
      and miracles and manifestations of the Spirit,
      or they threaten your unity and ministry
      by their arrogance in assuming they have received
            the Spirit in a certain way

and that this gives them special significance
    within your group.
These people must be lovingly but firmly dealt with
    lest they sabotage the power of God's Spirit
    in your midst and cripple your efforts to minister
    to your community.
God grant that they may repent and humble themselves
    under the mighty hand of God, and that they,
    in loving fellowship with you, will follow their
        Savior and Lord
    as He is revealed through the Holy Scriptures.

The Church at Thyatira:

Your congregation has lived through numerous crises
    in your persistent efforts to serve God
    and His wayward children throughout your community.
You have been faithful to the Word of God
    and have grown in the faith as you have creatively
    sought ways and means of reaching people about you.
While you are to be commended for this,
    there is one problem to which you must address yourself.
There is a person in your group who believes
    that she has received special vision
    and powers from God
    and who, contrary to the teachings of the Scriptures
    and the doctrines of the church, is proclaiming
    a very permissive sort of gospel among your members.
This woman has gone overboard
    in her immoral interpretation of Christian freedom
    in matters of worship and interpersonal relationships

and has prompted and encouraged promiscuity
in your midst.
She has been influenced by philosophies
and concepts outside of the church
that are contradictory to Christian beliefs and practices
and which are confusing some of your people.
She must be brought to judgment in this respect
before you lose any more members to her devious
manipulations
and, if she will not repent, must be excluded
from your fellowship.
Hold fast to what God's Word teaches you
and to what you have learned through your experiences
in your church and community.

The Church at Sardis:

Your congregation has done some spectacular things,
and the programs you have developed,
the things you have achieved, have become models
and goals for other churches throughout your province.
You have grown fat with success,
yet you have not really grown at all.
God has noted your good works;
but while many praise your numerous accomplishments,
the Spirit of God is sorely grieved.
According to God's diagnosis and judgment,
you, who have the reputation of being a live,
progressive, and rapidly growing congregation,
are in the process of dying.
You may be significant in the eyes of the world,
but the Lord of the church measures your effectiveness

by far different standards, and you sadly fail to
        measure up.
There is one thing only that prevents Him
        from lowering the boom upon you and your endeavors.
There is a small, and sometimes not so progressive,
        remnant within your congregation who have held to
        and lived by the true faith.
Unimpressed by the adulations and approbations
        directed to your congregation by their peers,
        they have discovered and committed themselves
        to the real meaning and purpose of discipleship
        and are therefore learning how to walk and serve
        in obedience to God and His will for their lives.
You had better take note of them, before it is too late,
        for they are those who are worthy of divine commendation,
        and they and their kind may yet be the salvation
        of your church.

The Church at Philadelphia:

You are truly a congregation
        in which the Spirit of Christ and God is present
        and is there accomplishing His eternal purposes.
You have little power in the eyes of the world,
        and the apparently successful churches around you
        take little note of your presence;
        yet God is with you and He will bless you
        with ever greater opportunities and responsibilities
        in the work of His kingdom.
The day will come when your sister churches,
        if they still exist, will recognize
        your valid contributions to the advancement

of the kingdom of God in this world
and, if they are to grow in spiritual effectiveness,
will begin to emulate you in their activities.
So do not be discouraged.
Continue as you have in God's Word—
making it the anchor and guiding star
of your life and activities.
Follow Jesus Christ as your Savior and Lord.
Let no one take from you what you have
or detour you away from the path you have chosen
to follow.
You will thereby escape God's judgment
upon the faithless and worldly significant
institutions
that fall far short of His standards,
and you will receive the crown of victory
in God's everlasting kingdom.

The Church at Laodicea:

God is well aware of your accomplishments.
As impressive as they may appear
in your estimation or even to the world about you,
they do not please the heart of God.
You may not earn the lowest marks
for your efforts; neither do they rank very high
in terms of spiritual value.
Whereas you are doing some good things
in response to God's Word to you,
you are neglecting those things
that are of greatest importance.

You believe fervently, for instance,
  in God's injunction to love your fellow human beings,
  yet you accommodate racist attitudes in your midst
  and allow prejudice and bigotry to exist amongst you.
You acknowledge the hunger and oppression that afflicts
  the suffering children of God throughout the world,
  yet you utilize your wealth and resources
  primarily for your own security and growth.
You zealously proclaim God's love and care
  and your need to respond in loving service,
  yet you take few risks or make no sacrifices
  in the course of Christian discipleship.
You know the destructive things that are going on
  in your community and nation, yet you dare not
  take issue with evil if such may endanger your income
  or your very existence.
You continue, however, to cheerfully commend yourselves
  as the chosen of God to serve Him in your community.
Should God reveal Himself even today,
  you would find your compromising attitudes
  and activities totally unacceptable to Him—
  that you have been more of a hindrance than a help
  in the building of His kingdom.
There is still time for repentance and renewal,
  time to be purged and refined by His fire,
  and time to dedicate your lives and activities
  to the accomplishment of His purposes
  and, in scorn of consequences, to be His beloved
  and loving servants in your world.
That time is now; tomorrow may be too late.

Revelation 4—7

What about that great day
    in which God's kingdom shall be revealed?
Is there any way in which we can picture
    this glorious event?
Some have had visions; others have dreamed dreams.
But it is not possible
    for our small minds to adequately visualize the glory
    of God's eternal kingdom.
Our images are earthbound.
Our words are like the babbling of babies.
Our imaginations are utterly incapable
    of grasping the majesty and beauty and power
    of that which awaits the children of God
    in that great Day.
We see but minute glimpses
    of His eternal glory in the elements about us,
    yet even these are beyond the comprehension
    of our finite thinking.
The pictures we compose are crooked lines
    or abstract blobs that only barely represent
        ultimate truth.

This, however, we believe: with the dawn
    of that magnificent day, Christ shall be revealed
    in all His glory and majesty.
All the hosts of heaven
    will be gathered to sing His praises.
And every human creature upon this earth,
    along with those who have gone on before us,

will know that this One who walked among us,
who revealed God's eternal love and who suffered
in His own body the consequences of our faithlessness
and disobedience, this One, the resurrected Christ,
is Lord and King of this world, the universe,
of heaven itself, for all eternity.
We live in a world that is subjected
to all kinds of atrocities.
Death and destruction shadow every living creature—
even the faithful children of God,
the inheritors of the new kingdom.
War, famine, the wickedness of powerful rulers,
the violence promulgated by insane men and women,
even the natural disasters that afflict this planet,
are perpetrated upon the just and the unjust,
the righteous and the unrighteous.
This is the world to which we have been entrusted
and in which we are commanded and empowered to serve.
Even while the prince of darkness enflames the hearts
and minds of his enslaved creatures and through them
wreaks destruction upon the sons and daughters of God,
God, Himself, through His Spirit, abides with us
and turns our suffering into something splendid
and makes even the martyrs' death a means
by which His purposes are advanced upon this earth.

This planet is not our eternal home.
The hour is rapidly approaching when Satan
and his deceived followers will lose their power
to harm and destroy and will themselves face
the wrath of the omnipotent and holy God.
They shall be cast into everlasting darkness
while the children of righteousness
shall be the citizens of God's kingdom forever.
God knows who we are—we who follow the Christ

who revealed Him to us.
He has placed His indelible brand upon us.
We belong to Him,
    and nothing or no one shall have the power
    to extricate us from His loving embrace.

Revelation 8—12

A contemporary pastor,
    frustrated over the tedious details
    of the parish ministry,
    weary and brain-sore in his struggle
    over the sermon for Sunday,
    propped his feet upon the desk
    and conjured up a vision.

He was on the beach of a seashore city.
Out across the waters a huge mushroom-like cloud,
    ever enlarging, coiled and boiled ominously over
        the ocean.
He was struck dumb with fear and immobilized
    with the realization that its death-dealing fumes,
    along with the tidal waves caused by this holocaust,
    would engulf the whole city behind him
    in a matter of a few hours.
When he finally came to himself
    he turned desperately to some of the mid-Sunday
    bathers and beachcombers and tried to tell them
    the meaning of the churning clouds.
He couldn't speak, not even whisper.
Kids digging in the sand,
    lovers embracing in the sun,
    swimmers romping in the surf,
    looked curiously at his arm-wavering antics
    and wide-open mouth, shook their heads,
    and went on with their activities.

Not making any impression upon the beachcrowd,
    he raced up into town with the frantic hope
    that he might arouse some responsible citizens
    to what was about to happen.
He ran in and out of stores
    but received only pathetic glances
    from busy shoppers collecting their weekly
        groceries.
The cop along main street was too busy issuing tickets
    for parking violations to pay any attention to him.
In residential areas, lawn mowers,
    car washers, and boat painters ignored him.
Bumper-to-bumper traffic honked, hooted,
    and hollered and almost ran him down
    as he attempted to attract their attention.

He finally ran out of breath
    and was about to resign himself
    to the agonizing futility of it all
    when he passed in front of a church.
The cloud over the ocean had blotted out the sun
    by now and the atmosphere was quiet and tense,
    like the calm before a storm
    or the dead center of a cyclone.
He decided that he could do little more
    than prepare his own soul for the inevitable,
    and so turned in and slipped into a back pew of
        the sanctuary.
An organ was playing.
Men and women in their best clothes
    lifted up their voices in a hymn of praise.
The minister began to speak.
The visitor's heart leaped in renewed hope
    as the man in the .pulpit calmly began

to tell the congregation about the very thing
he had been trying to get across to the people
on the beach and throughout the town.
The preacher intoned in a dead, dull manner
as if he didn't care a fig about what was about
to happen,
but his message, at least, was sincere and truthful.
Now the people would at least know and understand
and do something about this coming catastrophe.
But the people about him,
gazing attentively or nodding drowsily,
seemed hardly affected by the minister's words.

The sermon over, the benediction pronounced,
he sought out the pastor and vigorously pumped his hand
in gratitude, still unable to make any sound
come out of his own mouth.
The minister, obviously pleased that his sermon
had so profoundly impressed this strange visitor
that he couldn't speak a sound,
smiled graciously and sympathetically upon him.
He wandered almost unnoticed
among the departing worshipers, fully expecting
that they would be in a veritable panic,
or at least frantically making plans
to warn others and to evacuate the seashore city.
To his amazement they were all gathered about
in smug little cliques talking about
a million things—
dinner, business, children, relatives, vacations.
A group of men were comparing their golf scores.
A trio of girls were ogling a boy and giggling.
A quartet of women were informing themselves
on the latest developments in an old scandal.
A couple of ladies were making a point

of snubbing a third.
There were a few individuals
    who went directly to their cars
    and took off without speaking to anyone—
    probably because they were mad at somebody
    or because of something offensive
    in the sermon they had just heard.
By all appearances the minister's somber warnings
    about the coming disaster had no effect whatever
    upon the worshipers.

It was at this point
    that the pastor's feet slipped off the desk,
    almost toppling him from his chair.
He awakened and for a moment felt immersed
    in the horror of a great darkness,
    and like a clap of thunder,
    the voice of the Lord through the Old Testament
        prophet
    fell upon him in clarion and urgent intensity:
    "Whom shall I send, and who will go for Us?"
There was only a long silence.
There was no Isaiah to respond:
    "Here am I, O Lord, send me!"

Revelation 13—18

The judgment of God falls not only
     upon His creatures who inhabit this world,
     but upon the institutions that they create.
Every nation upon this globe is judged
     as ancient Babylon was judged.
Over against the wickedness of Babylon
     is the righteousness of Jerusalem—the remnant,
     redeemed by Jesus Chrst, which persists,
     even within the institutions that seek to control them
     to follow and serve their Redeemer and King.
All authorities, corporations, bureaucracies,
     ideologies, traditions, and institutions,
     shall be called to account before the judgment
          of God.
Whatever their motives for existence,
     whatever their contributions to humanity's existence
     and benefit, they bear the stamp of depravity;
     they become, for the most part, the very enemies
          of God's kingdom.
Many of them are necessary to our present existence—
     and are often used by God to further His purposes,
     but they will never become a part of God's great kingdom
     in that great day when He shall be revealed.

The church itself, as an institution,
     has fallen far short of God's holy standards,
     and has often become like a harlot—
     abusing God's eternal love to relate promiscuously
     to foreign loves or lovers,

or obscuring God's message of redeeming love
among its constituents and ignoring His commands
to bring healing and hallowing
to His human creatures throughout the world.
Whereas we have found the institutional church
necessary to our faith as God's children,
it has often been a thorn in God's side
and inhibited the accomplishment of His purposes
on this planet.

Yet even within the Babylon
of the institutional church there is Jerusalem—
the faithful remnant who shall greet Christ's coming
and His everlasting kingdom with joy.
God knows who they are,
and while the institutions which men create
fall under His judgment,
there shall come out of these institutions
those who bear upon them the brand
of God's redeeming grace, and they shall live forever
as the citizens of His eternal kingdom.

Revelation 19—22

This is not the time for despair;
  it is the time for celebration!
Jesus has come;
    He is present with us amidst the trials
    and tribulations of this tempestuous world;
    He is about ready to come again
    and to gather together His faithful followers
        into the fully revealed and eternally reigning
        kingdom of God.
The "marriage supper of the Lamb" is about to take place,
    and the suffering, celebrating, faithful children of God
    of all nations and generations are invited.
Christ will, once and for all time,
    reveal Himself as the living, overcoming, victorious
    Lord of heaven and earth.
Evil will be eradicated;
    all stumbling blocks will be removed;
    those who oppose God and His people will be overcome;
    the spiritual forces of evil will be bound
        and destroyed.
Sorrow will turn to joy, night into day.
Tears will give way to laughter;
    ugliness will yield to beauty.
Wars will cease and peace shall encompass people
    and nations, and all the world will recognize
    and give honor to the eternal kingdom of our Lord.
It is on this great day that the suffering martyrs,
    the struggling saints, the priests and prophets,
    servants and disciples of all the ages

shall be united together to sing their praises
to their eternal Savior and King.
Words cannot describe it—this fantastic event
about to take place.
But God's faithful children—
clothed in His righteousness—
can believe it and hope for it
and ready themselves for it,
because it will happen,
and all the pain and suffering
that encompassed them in this world
will be forgotten in the glorious
revelation of Christ as King
in the world to come.
Jesus is about to return and take His church to Himself.
He is coming soon!
Let us begin the celebration even now!